CW00798209

The Allotment

....CONTINUED!

The eagerly anticipated sequel to the critically acclaimed The Allotment!

By Jethro Le' Roy

Also available in this series:

The Allotment!

The Allotment....Reprisal!.

Dalyn Publishing
Dalyn House
270 Lower Hillmorton Rd
Rugby CV21 4AE
Enquiries, comments, ideas and submissions to:
dwfurlong@talktalk.net

By the same author:
John Slater: The Journey
John Slater: The German Job
And the   popular   Oh Grumps! Series of children's books
Available in paperback or Kindle format from Amazon.

Penny: My Constant Companion
and Friend. I Miss You, Mate

The Allotment!.....Continued!

I just heard the tail end of the conversation as I walked up the path.

" ....and he hears some really good boogey-woogey music as he goes past. He goes in and there is this little guy –he's only about a foot tall – playing a little piano on the pub counter. He listens and then says "Wow, that's amazing. Where did he come from?"

The bartended pulls a little button out of his pocket. "I found this on the floor this morning" he explained. "If you look you can see the words 'Rub and wish" inscribed on it. Well, I rubbed and wished and this guy showed up."

"Big Mick" McAvoy might have been a big, fat, - sorry, not pc, make that big boned - scruffily dressed bloke but he could tell a good joke. The other guys were hanging on to his every word.

"The guy takes the button from the bartender. 'Can I have a go?' The bartender nods and the customer rubs the button. Suddenly, the pub is full of dogs. 'No, no, that's not what I wished for. I wanted a hundred pounds not a hundred hounds.'

The bartender looked at him. 'You really think that I asked for a 12 inch pianist?'

Everyone burst out laughing. I had obviously joined a joke telling session.

I'm always envious of a person who can not only tell a good joke but can remember them as well. I can hear a great joke and have forgotten it by the time I want to tell someone.

I guess that is what is meant by the term Old Timers Disease. You get old and then you forget things.

You walk into a room and forget why. They find you on the landing with a confused look on your face.

You mistake the built in wardrobe for the toilet. No? Just me then. Don't worry, the wife puts newspaper down in there now. You're halfway through a sentence and forget the rest of what you wanted to say. Now...... where was I?

Oh yeah, walking up the path. The main path between the plots on the Victory Allotments.

The Victory Allotments are council run, were started during World War 2 and have continued ever since. The land involved covers two acres and consists of around forty plots.

The actual number fluctuates because some large plots are split into half and some half plots became large plots again.

Basically, a new tenant was given the choice of a half or a large plot. The more ambitious, their enthusiasm fuelled by the countless gardening shows on tv, go for a large plot.

The timid, the infirm or the "I'll see how it goes" types had half plots. If they liked having an allotment they sometimes then took over an adjacent half plot.

But, mostly people just got fed up and left and the whole cycle started over again.

Ironically, it was the tv programmes that were to blame for people leaving as well as getting an allotment.

Just imagine the scene. You are at home watching some poncey tv gardener showing how things are done. The allotment plot is prepared in half an hour and the first crops all planted by Part Two.

The next programme shows happy families cheerfully gathering their harvest and proudly bearing it home. Cue beaming expressions and motivating music.

Proud potatoes, perfect peas, sweet yellow corn, eye watering onions, blood dripping beetroots, perfect parsnips, luscious lettuce, canny cabbages –sorry, got a bit stuck on that one – and, oh, ….you probably get the picture.

Everything perfect, grown to perfection and tasting like Ambrosia on the tongue. And healthy. So healthy that there should be a law against it.

The reality was slightly different. In the real world the plot was overgrown with tall grasses, voracious stinging nettles, rambling brambles and the ridges left from the previous tenant's unsuccessful attempts to clear, dig and tame it.

Many blistered hands, blunt shears, kaput strimmers, barrowloads of rubbish and an ocean of sweat and grime later, you have cleared your plot. Take a moment of pride to reflect on that success. That was only Round One. The warm up. The Prelude.

Round Two consisted of digging your plot over. If you thought about it beforehand, you purchased a load of manure from the local farmer, spread that about and then dug it in at the same time.

You start with one corner. Dig, turn, beat, dig again. You look up towards the far, the very far, end.

You have the sudden, sobering, thought that this large tract of real estate is going to be transformed with only your dilapidated fork, your bleeding hands and numbed and bruised feet.

You carry on. Day after day. In all weather. Until, finally, you are at the other end and turning the last, the very last, forkful of earth.

You have done it. You have dug your patch.

At about this time, the whisper of reality is starting to hover on the horizon. You look proudly at the big patch of bare, dug, earth that you have wrestled from the wilderness.

You then look at your blistered hands , bloodied nails, feel your broken back and get just a hint, a little whiff, of the task you have really set yourself . Reality bites small chunks out of you at first then increasingly larger ones.

You are suddenly thinking that Bloody Alan from the tv doesn't know what he is talking about and is really what the first three letters of his surname suggest.

But, stick with it if you have the heart, the nerve and the stamina. Persevere and you get muscles, an eight pack –early days yet – and a resemblance of fitness.

Become immune to aching muscles, a snappy wife, a blazing sun, freezing mornings and weary evenings and week-ends. Firmly push that little niggle out of your mind.

Ignore the little voice that whispers seductively in your ear and suggests that it would be much easier to just go to Aldi and buy the bloody stuff.

Battle on, plant your seed, - I can think of nicer ways to plant my seed - tend your plot and carry on when others have fallen by the wayside. Work from Can See to Can't See.

Fight the weather, the marauding insects, the failed crops. Carry on when lesser men have fallen by the roadside and, if you do all of this, then, and only then, you will become an Allotmenteer, my son.

Alternatively, you could be like me and take over someone's well tended plot. That's what I did. Bugger all that pioneering stuff. That's too much like hard work.

The assorted bunch of blokes telling jokes and tall stories are, have become, my mates. There are four of them and we call ourselves the Allotmenters. One for All and All for One and all that crap.

Of course there are more than we few, we precious few, we band of brothers on the Victory Allotments. But we are the closest in that we are both plot neighbours and members of a secret society. And, no, I can't tell you about that. It's a secret.

There is the aforementioned Big Mick McAvoy. He is called Big Mick, not on account of his big boneyness but because there used to be a Little Mick.

Little Mick left last year but a continuous supply of Gregg's finest products has ensured that the Big part of Mick's name seems somehow appropriate.

Mick works as a van driver on parcel deliveries. He used to work for Eddy Stobart but left on "health" reasons.

Some said it was because he needed a forklift to get into his truck cab. Others said it was because the groove left in his belly by the steering wheel went so deep as to be deemed dangerous. Whatever the reason, he was let go for Health and Safety reasons.

In his mid thirties, he has a quick temper, a closely cropped head, a huge thirst, a gigantic appetite and an endless supply of fairly clean jokes.

Paul Tiler is an average height, thin, non-descript sort of guy. He is a retired mechanic and mechanics are always good guys to have on your team. He is always shabbily dressed with a flat cap on his head.

His face is deeply lined and deeply tanned. The latter clearly in evidence when he removes his hat to wipe the sweat off his bald head. There is a very defined white Plimsoll line across his forehead.

Paul doesn't say much but what he does say is worth listening to. He is the "Go To" guy for allotment related advice and information.

Peter Wills is a tall, mid-sixties stout guy with a ruddy complexion and a good head of swept back grey hair.

You tend to notice hair when your own starts to get thinner and thinner. When you realise that the pain on top of your head is sunburn and your forehead keeps getting bigger.

He worked for a large, local engineering firm for most of his adult life. When the company relocated to China, he decided that the daily commute would be a tad too much so he accepted a thick wad of redundancy money.

As his hobby was engineering, clocks and locks, he used the money to set up a locksmith business. Over twenty years, he expanded this into a ten vehicle, seventeen staff and a trade and retail counter business. He officially retired two years ago and the business is now run by his two sons.

Adrian Miles is a widower. He lost his wife to cancer five years back and it is only the allotment and our company that, we suspect, keeps him from thinking of joining her.

Adrian is a small, trim, guy. The type of guy who always looks immaculate. One of those Teflon guys who are impervious to dirt and grime. Put him in a white suit, roll him in a dung heap and he would always come up clean and sparkling. One of those guys.

As clean and sparkling as a diamond in a dung heap as the toilet paper ad has it.

He also is mid sixties, has sharp features and inquisitive eyes. His most distinctive feature is his thick, snow white, hair which is set off by a deeply tanned face.

For some strange unknown reason women, my wife Lynne included, seem to go mad for his white hair.

Adrian used to be an accountant for a large company.

Big Mick, Paul Tiler, Pete Wills and Adrian Miles. One, two, three, four. Only one left in this group of Super Heroes that is The Allotmenteers to introduce you to.

The jewel in the crown, the pick of the bunch, the dog's gonads. Ladies and Gentlemen, I give you.......Dave Williams.

Yours truly. Retired ex truck driver, owner operator and transport journalist.

Sixty seven years young. Devastatingly handsome, the body of an athlete. A mere ten inches short of six foot six. A veritable babe magnet. A leg-end in his own mind.

Prone to bouts of short sightedness and inflated self worth.

So, that is us. We are the Allotmenteers and this...... this is our story.

Chapter Two.

After a few more increasingly dirtier jokes, we broke up. Wandered back to our own plots. Retreated into our respective sheds and pondered on Life, Love and the true meaning of the universe. Anything to put off the moment when we might have to do some actual work on our patches.

But, to be fair, there wasn't that much to do in February. Most of the clean up stuff had been done in October and November.

A few sheltered and hardy raspberries had survived to provide a bit of colour for Christmas. The winter cabbage and brussel sprouts had elicted gasps of surprise and wonderment as they were served up for Christmas dinner.

But, basically the allotments slumbered during the winter months. I used to walk down regularly with my little Yorkie, Zak, and keep an eye on things.

Zak's mum, Penny, used to accompany me but now prefers to stay at home and sleep. She, like me, is getting on a bit so I understand. Unfortunately Lynne won't let me do the same.

I do hope that, next time, I come back as a dog. They seem to have it so much easier. Especially in our house.

Adrian's bungalow, along with those of several other plot holders, overlooked the allotments so there were plenty in the neighbourhood who became Allotment Watchers.

As for the others, well, I guess they hibernated. During a few of the relatively warmer days, they could sometimes be spotted scurrying about foraging and blinking furiously in the weak sunlight.

Actually, I quite liked the winter rest period. Zak and I walked around the allotments enjoying the crisp frosty air, the crunch of frozen grass underfoot and the fascinating spectacle of the frost laden spider webs with the low sun shining on them.

I looked out for any damage caused by the weather or the occasional vandal. Some people also tend to think of allotments as a sort of free vegetable supermarket.

We tend to get a lot of pilfering in the summer months when everything is growing.

During the winter we find that sheds have sometimes been broken into. No doubt the vandals are looking for tools or anything else they can find and sell on.

But as most of us take anything of value home for the winter period, the only real annoyance is having to repair the forced entry or get a new padlock.

My kingdom is about halfway down the path leading to the Back gate. This gate is normally used by people, such as myself, who live in easy walking distance of the allotments.

There is a Front gate with car park but that is down on the bottom half of the allotments. To get to that I would have to walk past the Bottom gate so, unless I bring a vehicle down, I always use the Bottom gate.

The allotments themselves are divided by location. The top half is a main path with plots on either side. Naturally, my plot is in the prestigious top half.

The Bottom half is the same layout but on a slope. Hence top and bottom location. The bottom half also tends to be wetter with several plots unusable because of the water permanently on them.

The council did briefly consider letting these waterlogged plots out to some of the Chinese families in our area. I think the idea went along the lines of.. "Chinese? Water logged land. Rice paddies. They'll love it". They obviously didn't because as yet, we have no Chinese people in residence.

So, that's a brief outline of what the Victory Allotments are like. Pretty much like any other allotment anywhere in the land.

Any bunch of people working in a confined space has the potential for trouble and we have certainly had ours.

But, at the moment, I am gasping for a cuppa so I'll get back to that subject later on.

I was dead lucky getting my allotment. A chance encounter with a neighbour in Aldi was the reason.

He was boasting about having an allotment and, after I asked him if there were any vacancies, told me there was a way round the waiting list.

Long story short, I ended up with his. That was a year ago and I have been enjoying the fruits of his labour ever since.

My patch of heaven has a relatively new chainlink fence around three sides and is bordered by a hedge at the top end.

Because the plot came to me with raised beds, I have kept them. Some say they are better, some not. For me, they work because they save me work.

Mine are made from scaffolding poles and boards. Two full size boards on each long side and two half boards at the ends.

Four cut down poles at each end and two in the middles, driven into the ground, act as supports. They are then filled with earth and are ready to go.

The benefits are that they save bending down, save digging and are easily covered with netting or plastic to keep the bugs or weather away. A quick muck and fork over each spring and that's the preparation done.

The disadvantages, say the diehards, are the waste of space. In that respect they are probably right.

Mine are slabbed all round and the only bit of open ground is at the top where I grow spuds and a few raspberries.

So, yes, they do waste a lot of useable ground. But are easily maintained and to keep neat and tidy. And, if you are not growing stuff for a large family there is more than enough growing area for what Lynne and I require. Even including the stuff, a lot of stuff, we give away to family and friends.

I should also add that my benefactor had several beefy men come in and get the allotment into shape for him. They cleared the ground, put up the raised beds and did the fencing and slabbing.

He even had his house gardener come and work on the plot. Mind you, she was young, pretty and willing but not a very good gardener. He eventually got divorced, married her and left the area. Hence me getting his allotment.

I also have a nice shed to go with my raised beds. It was new last autumn and replaced the one that got burnt down. That's also on the list of " I'll get back to that later" stuff.

That torched one was an 12 foot by 8 foot deluxe with porch and veranda. More a summer house than shed.

The guy I got it off had it equipped with single bed, carpet, pictures on the wall and a tv and radio run off the solar panels on the roof.

Mine is a more modest six by six but it suits me.

Most of the sheds on the allotments were second hand or self built with varying degrees of competence Along the lines of "I have all this spare wood, what can I do with it? I know I'll build a shed." type of thinking.

I tried to get a good second hand one but, in the end, got a good deal on this one with free delivery and erection included.

Lynne got all excited about the latter until I explained. She took it very well, I thought.

I put it on the site of the torched one and this gave me a good slabbed patio area.

I had also bought a 6' x6' greenhouse off a departing Goodlifer who had 'enough of this self sufficiency malarkey'. I sited this on the slabbing near the shed.

Inside the shed, I had some plastic chairs rescued from my daughter's. There were only a few tools on the rack inside. I would bring more down as the season progressed.

I had my faithful gas stove that had accompanied me in the cab when I was a Super-Hero type international trucker. I had cups, tea bags, coffee, sugar, a water container and a radio.

There is always something nice about sitting outside in the early mornings or late evenings. No one about. A cup of tea and surrounded by nature.

The bird songs, the wind in the trees or just a heavy silence as the earth woke up or settled in for the night.

At the far end of the allotments was the raised mound of the West Coast Mainline railway embankment.

It ran from London Euston through the Midlands and up North to exotic locations like Crewe and Liverpool.

 It even ventured over Hadrian's Wall and into the foreign wastelands of Scotland.

Home to the Deep Fried Battered Mars Bar clans. Home of hunters and hunts for the elusive Haggis. A tiny, furry creature that had the legs on one side of its body shorter than the other. Yes, I did ask the question: apparently it is so they can scuttle up and down hills sideways.

 I used to watch each train go by and pity the crammed occupants as they started their working day with an increasingly hectic daily commute.

I often saluted them from my patio with a raised cuppa and the thought that retirement wasn't all bad.

The water boiled and I poured it into two cups. Added tea bags, powdered milk and waited for my almost daily guest.

Chapter Three.

I had just dunked and removed the tea bags, added the grey powdered milk mixture when Adrian arrived and, as he always did, knocked on the door.

We had been doing this morning cuppa ritual for some time now but he always knocked. He was the kind of guy who always observed the niceties and etiquette of us older generation types. A diamond shining in a dung heap kind of guy.

"In or out?" I asked. Sometimes if the weather was a bit off we sat inside. Sometimes we talked, sometimes we sat in companionable silence, enjoying our drink and our surroundings.

"Outside" he decided. Good choice. Even though it was mid-February, it was a nice morning.

One of those unexpected winter mornings when you think the winter is over and then wake up to crotch deep snow the next morning.

He dragged two plastic chairs onto the slabbed patio area and we sat facing the allotments. We drank, looked and listened.

There were a few early bird allotmenteers pottering about. Repairing any damage caused by last month's strong winds. Doing a bit of clearing up, weeding, avoiding the missus or just glad to be back on site after a relatively mild winter.

Adrian cleared his throat, drank, looked at me, cleared his throat. This went on for a while. Clearly he had something on his mind. Eventually he decided to speak.

"You're happily married aren't you?" he asked. Wow, that came out of the blue.

Happily married? Was I happily married? Lynne and I had married in '67 so that made 48 years. Happy? I guess we were comfortable with each other. We had grown used to each other. I thought of her as my best friend. I guess, I hoped, she felt the same. Would I miss her? Yes, definitely. So that answered that question.

"Yes, I suppose we are. We have had our ups and downs. A few shouting matches, sulks and walk-outs but we still get along. Probably more to my being away for long periods when I was on the road more than anything else. Absence makes the heart grow fonder and all that. Why do you ask?"

" I guess I'm a bit down." He replied as he avoided my gaze.

"Today would have been my 45th anniversary and tomorrow it will be six years since Gwen passed.

I always get a bit melancholy this time of the year." His voice grew sadder and softer. "You know, Spring, new beginnings and all that. She loved this time of year. And….. and… I guess I just miss her……" His voice broke and his shoulders slumped. His mouth was moving but nothing came out.

All of which posed a dilemma for me. What should I do? My first instinct was to put my arm around his shoulder My second instinct was to do nothing. My gut told me the latter was right. At least I hoped it was.

Adrian and I, in fact all of the Allotmenteers with the exception of Big Mick, were of the same age and generation.

You know, the Stiff Upper Lip generation. The Show No Emotion to Other Men less people think you are "queer" generation.

The late 40's post war baby boomers who tried unsuccessfully and uncomfortably to bridge the gap between the old Victorian generation and the new thrusting 'get rid of all that old fashioned crap' generation.

The old timers who rarely swore in a world full of almost automatic swearing. The granddads who are both horrified and in awe of their grandchildren. At what they could and do achieve and what they had lost in values.

The Trying Generation who tried to make sure their children had a better home life than they did. A home life where a hug to a crying child was permitted. A life of praise for the under achiever as well as the gifted.

A life where parents, especially fathers, were permitted to show emotion, shed a tear and show love to their offspring without the old in-built emotionless values of their parents dictating every move and mood.

So bugger my gut. I, who could not remember ever being kissed or hugged by my parents, turned to my Oldtimer friend and held him in my arms.

Held him as he cried out his grief, anguish and loneliness. Held him whilst my own tears flowed freely. Held him in full view of the allotment and didn't bloody care.

Afterwards, we sat in silence. Adrian finished his tea. Stood up and gave me a half embarrassed and half "Thanks Mate" tug of a smile and left.

Subject closed. Never to be mentioned again. What happened on the allotment stayed on the allotment. Allotmenteer Rules.

Chapter Three

The "Polish shop" as it was known locally, was at the end of a five shop row on Downybed Road.

The owner was a Polish man who had emigrated to Rugby a few years back.

Rugby was, seemingly, rapidly becoming an off-shoot district of Warsaw.

This was due mainly to the high labour requirements of the multitude of Big Shed warehousing complexes nibbling away at the green fields surrounding the town.

Labour requirements that our fellow EEC Polish neighbours flocked to fill. Polish had almost become our second language.

You could be standing in a queue in a Rugby shop and you would suddenly hear someone speaking in English. The incident was so rare and unexpected that you could only stand and stare. It was like being abroad and hearing your native tongue again.

Living in Rugby was getting to be similar to being on an extended holiday in Poland.

Don't get me wrong. I have nothing against the Polish. They are hard working, agreeable and well mannered on the whole.

Also a butt for many jokes. Jokes along the lines of "What does an English bride get from her Polish husband on her wedding day that is long and hard?.......A new surname."

Anyway, the owner of the "Polish Shop" was an ex international truck driver like myself. I knew that from visiting his shop and because he had an allotment on the Victory allotments.

He got fed up of being on the road and decided to come to England where many, if not most, of his friends and relatives were now living.

Like most truck drivers, he is a highly intelligent, salt of the earth type of caring and likeable person.

He quickly sussed that warehouse work wasn't for him. He analysed and decided that Rugby, because of its location, road and rail links was the place to be.

He drove around the area and spotted this empty shop. He decided that its ex council house estate location was ideal. So, he took a gamble, a largish loan from his family and opened shop, so to speak.

Using his truck driving connections he began importing Polish foodstuffs to sell alongside the more traditional and staid foodstuff his English customers expected and asked for.

After about a year he found that he was getting more and more fellow country men buying his 'home from home' goods. Also that many of the locals were developing a taste for the good quality but cheaper "foreign" stuff.

Competing with the Indian shop on the end of the row for "English" foods wasn't good business sense. So he decided to concentrate – apart from staples like milk and tea – on his developing import food goods and to expand into the more familiar and profitable Polish household cleaning products.

As a sideline, he got an allotment and began growing and selling both familiar and unfamiliar vegetables.

At the other end of the row was the afore mentioned "proper" local shop selling papers and the other necessities of life.

It was also a post office and a collection place for sending parcels through the Hermes distribution system. Naturally, it was run by a hard working Indian family. It wouldn't have been deemed a proper English shop otherwise.

Two other buildings housed a computer shop and a well stocked diy, bits and bobs –for all those things you had forgotten or couldn't be bothered to go into town for – Aladdin's cave sort of place.

The remaining establishment was a well frequented and loved chippy.

The essentials to any sort of proper English lifestyle and gastronomic aspirations.

Conveniently, there was a large Old Folks home on the other side of the road. Here our well loved, respected and venerated old folk resided, carried on, played bingo and tried to enjoy what little life they had left.

A steady stream of shuffling, frame walking, carpet slippered and unsteady elderly inhabitants crossed back and forth between the shops and their retirement home.

Some times one or two made a concerted break for freedom. Mainly short lived after the guards and dogs were unleashed. But most accepted their lot and patiently waited for the old guy with the scythe and cloak to come calling on them.

My ever loving Lynne had, for some time now, been suggesting that I might "like to have a quick look round and see what it was like" type tour of the retirement facility.

 Whether for herself or me wasn't made clear. However, I have begun to strongly suspect the latter.

To cut down on the potential accidents and the endless queues of impatiently waiting vehicles, there was a Crossing Lady.

And, not just any Crossing Lady. This large boned, ruddy faced, lolly pop wielding defender of the old and infirm, hated cars with a passion.

It has been rumoured that, on her bad days, she would chase them up and down the road.

However, I don't listen to rumours. But, she did have this "I'm in command here" attitude that made her pick her moments to act. The road could have been perfectly clear with no traffic in sight but that wouldn't do.

She would round up her charges into a milling, impatient, dribbling, confused and toothless pack. Snapping and snarling, she circled them and kept the circle tight. She waited….and waited.

Gazing up and down the deserted road she listened. With sniffing nose pointed to the sky and ears revolving like antennae, she waited.

When she had sighted her prey, she waited until the last possible moment before jumping into the middle of the road, mighty shield held aloft and bingo winged arm pointing an accusing sausage sized finger. Then, raking the hapless driver with her ice cold gaze, she would herd her charges across.

Fifteen minutes later, when her charges were safely ensconced in the various shops, she would grudgingly, yet regally, wave the fuming but cowed driver on.

Lollypop Ladies, eh? They make me cross.

Just further down the road was a large recreation field. Here people walked their dogs, neglected to pick up after them and dumped their litter.

Recently the council had, at great and opposed expense, created a skate board and mountain bike facility here.

It consisted of huge drainage pipes, concrete ramps, towering inclines and the other essentials that skaters and bikers needed to let off steam.

It also became the rallying point for the hordes of nocturnal young people to gather, plan and plot.

When there was a large enough number, these Play Station mercenaries would shuffle, zombie-like, up towards the shops.

There, contrary to local council expectations, was where they preferred to gather and play.

Harassing the shop customers, intimidating the elderly, picking their bags, shoplifting and being generally obnoxious being their chosen methods of letting off steam and maturing into responsible adults.

The shop keepers would complain about the shoplifting. Local residents would complain about the noise, bad language and litter.

The elderly residents from across the road would never venture out alone. So the Care Home manager would complain to the council.

Complaints that seemed to fall on deaf ears.

The Indian shop owner purchased a device aimed primarily at the young. This was basically a loud speaker mounted outside that played irritating noises that, supposedly, only young ears could hear.

Eventually, the purpose was, the suitably irritated and annoyed group of youths would move away out of earshot.

It worked for a while until the Care Home manager found out what had been causing his patients headaches, panic attacks and to remove their super efficient hearing aids.

End of deterrent system. The old folk across the road provided a sizeable chunk of the shop business so the whispering "noises in my head" inducing speaker was removed.

Occasionally, the police and council would have an all out effort to stop the packs of bored youngsters massing but, mainly, it persisted. The local shops and shoppers began to despair.

Obviously, everyone agreed, it had to be stopped but how?

It was beginning to look like a "When you have a problem, who you gonna call?" type of situation.

Chapter Four

I didn't do much more. I checked around, put my tea making stuff away and locked the shed. Time to go home. Another busy day on the allotment.

Because I wanted to go to the shop for a paper, I headed down to the Front gate. This was a double metal model with mesh and a warning "CCTV operates in this area" sign.

It was all a con. There was no cctv. No proper security at all. The chain link fence that supposedly surrounded the allotment had been breached in several places after failing to resist the all-out attacks of persistent vegetable thieves.

Directly opposite the front gate was a fenced off area. There was a white picket fence, a grassed section and a sturdy shelter.

We used it as a quiet, contemplative area. We had all chipped in with labour, materials and money. It was a haven and, more importantly, as a plaque on the inside showed, a memorial.

And, yes, it is also on the "I'll get back to that later" list. Be patient. I have to be in the mood to dredge up those kind of memories.

I crossed the main road and walked up to the shops in Downybed Road. There was an aggro of youths milling around outside. I ignore their 'Grandad' comments, requests for change, was I looking for business? and similar before pushing my way into the Indian shop.

I got the local paper, the Rugby Advertiser, and handed over my money and voiced my usual "it gets thinner and thinner" complaint.

I quite often threaten to stop buying it as we get a free Observer and Review in the evening. The latter is a scaled down version of the Advertiser.

But Lynne always tells me to "get an Advertiser on the way back" and, being uncomfortable with her sulks and moans if I don't, I comply.

I called into the Polish shop on my way past. Jan Hawkn'spit – not his real surname but easier to pronounce without the effort and all that dribbling – the owner, greeted me cheerfully.

There was a standing bet that Jan would give the first English person to pronounce his surname, to his satisfaction, a bottle of good whiskey.

His full name is Januariusz Czernianski. He hadn't parted with any of his whiskey as yet.

Being a German speaker, which is similar to Polish, I once tried to work it out and the nearest I could get in English was "The brave, ex truckdriver, warrior who crosses the fierce sea to trade with the natives."

I have a sneaking suspicion that many overlong european words or names are there simply to confuse we easily impressed English.

Like the German word Dona-danpff-schif-farthts-gesellschafts(I had to put the breaks in to fit it in) which means Danube Steamship company Captain.

Mind you, we have our own home grown word silliness.

Like the Welsh place name of:

Llanfairpwllgwyngyllgogerychwyrndobwyllllantys iliogogoochCompare.

AKA The Church of Mary in the Hollow of the whitehazel near a rapid whirlpool and the church of Saint Tysilio near the Red Cave. That similarly trips off the tongue doesn't it?

You might be interested to know, or not, that it is a made up word combining different locations for a publicity gimmick in the 1860's. And you thought the Welsh didn't like a laugh. People who wear a national dress like theirs have definitely got to have a sense of humour.

Jan is an energetic and likeable guy in his 40's. Tall, thin and always working in the shop or the allotment.

"Hello Boss" he said. He calls everyone boss. I think he has problems pronouncing difficult English surnames like Smith or Jones. "How are you? Everything okey-dokey?"

"Hi Jan. Yes. Just come from the allotment, got my Advertiser and going home. How are you keeping? Everything ok?"

"Cushty bro, cushty." Jan watches a lot of Only Fools and Horses repeats. I think he thinks that we all speak like that.

Someone down the allotment once taught him that a good adjective to use was "Bollocking" so we tend to get a lot of bollocking from Jan as well. But, he is a great bloke and gets on well with everyone.

"Apart from those bollocking kids who are always hanging about outside causing trouble" he finished.

After he had finished complaining about those "bollocking kids" the conversation drifted towards the allotment.

He asked me how the Tool Co-op idea I had last year was coming along.

Most of the allotment holders had their own basic tools. Shovels, forks, that kind of thing.

I had the idea that a co-operative where we jointly purchased the more exotic tools like rotovators, industrial strimmers, lawn mowers and small tillers would benefit everyone. Everyone would chip in and share the tools equally on an 'as and when' basis.

It had a mixed reaction. The people with their own rotovators and stuff didn't see the point. The half plotters didn't want to pay the same rate as the full plotters. Some wanted priority. Some wanted to know where the items would be kept. And would they be safe? What happened if they left? Would they get anything back?

Basically, there were as many Fors as Againsts. But, those of us in the first catergory, were still leaning towards a tool sharing project.

Jan was all for it and mentioned that he could get some high end Stihl gear at the right bollocking price from home. Home being, presumably, Poland. "Luvely Jubbly." as he described it.

I told him I would arrange an allotment meeting to discuss it when the weather warmed up and enough people would attend.

I left the shop and went home. I still had a list of household To-Do things and wanted to cross some of them off. For some reason though, the list never seemed to get any smaller.

I sometimes had the sneaking thought that I had a saboteur at home. Hold that thought.

Entering the front path I had the satisfied thought that the front gate didn't lean anymore. I had eventually got round to sorting it after putting it off for some time. I don't know why because it proved relatively simple to fix.

Now we don't have the hassle of supporting the gate as we try to close it. Nobody ever closed it anyway so I couldn't see the point of having it. So now we don't. More modern and trendy. If only all my jobs were so simple to cross of the To Do list.

Lynne and I live on Victory Drive. It is in the Hillmorton area and considered one of the better locations in Rugby.

 Better in that it was started after the second War and built to a quality and not a price.

The houses were well built with substantial gardens and good shops and a pub nearby.

 It was once a drive but then expanded and widened and is now one of the main routes into the town.

The section where we live is on a section of dual carriageway.

 The grass central reservation supports a selection of trees which somehow survive on a combined mix of poor drainage and carbon monoxide fumes from the passing traffic.

This puts our opposite neighbours a good distance apart. But, because the road slopes down from the opposite houses, it also creates a 'them and us' mentality. Because the opposite neighbours look down on us geographically, they also tend to look down on us status wise.

There is no difference in the houses, quality or prices except for that slight elevation.

But, if someone in Rugby asks where you live and you say Victory Drive the next question is invariably High Side or Low Side?

A complete reversal of my status as a Top End allotmenteer as opposed to a Bottom Ender. But such is life. It giveth and it taketh away.

On the plus side, the house is bought and paid for. The kids have flown the nest and, apart from a steadily decreasing number of old Yorkies, Lynne and I have it to ourselves.

Sometimes we can go for weeks without actually having to speak to each other. Lynne reckons that, when I put my mind to it, I could sulk for England. But, apart from having space between us if we want it, we generally rub along nicely.

We work together with the mutual respect and understanding of long term partners.

She tells me what to do and I do it. Simples.

Even the House and I have finally reached an understanding. When I first came off the road and retired, the House resented me. It wasn't used to me. It was used to Lynne getting skilled and expensive people in to administer to its every need.

It couldn't accept that every man with a toolbox has untapped, unrecognised and, as yet, undiscovered house tending skills.

Whatever I tried to do, it sabotaged my efforts. Freshly hung wallpaper hung down in spirals when I turned my back.

Woodwork contorted and twisted to make it look like I hadn't put it up straight.

Electricity showed its resentment by blowing fuses whenever I fiddled with it.

But, gradually, over time, the House has mellowed. It has accepted that I am here to stay. It doesn't fight back anymore.

It let me put up the decking without too much of a fight. However, it did have the last laugh when Lynne leaned on the balustrade and it fell over.

Not my fault. The House should have reminded me that it still needed to be securely screwed on.

It hasn't given up completely though. It still tries to give the impression that it is my diy skills that have improved and not that it has taken my threat to sell it seriously.

So, I was feeling pretty content that February morning. The allotment waking up for the season. The House finally mellowing. Lynne.....well, baby steps and all that.

In the kitchen, I put the kettle on. The blight of my life was in her room. Her room is packed to the ceiling with the necessities of her crafting hobby. To the extent that, when the local crafting shop runs out of anything, its manager calls Lynne first to see if she has it. She usually does

Because of the space problem there is only room for one easy chair and one desk chair. She uses the former for hobby stuff and the latter for swearing at the computer stuff.

Computer stuff being on-line games, Facethingy, Twatter or restocking craft supplies from Amazon.

I have my own room. Mine is green and restful. Lynne's is yellow and supposedly calming. Although her language, as she shouts at her computer for being slow, does seem to disprove Lawrence Le Really Boring's so called expert theory and advice.

So far she hasn't shouted at me for being slow. But, some nights, she does look up from her book to rather impatiently ask "haven't you finished yet?"

My room is also slightly larger so I have two reclining armchairs, a good music system and a large 44inch plasma screen on the wall. I was allowed that because it was second hand – make that pre-owned – from Ebay. As was my computer and, thinking about it, practically everything else in the room.

Well, why buy new when second hand is just as good, sometimes better, and a lot cheaper?

Now, before you jump to the conclusion that we live a completely separate existence to each other I must point out that we do have a communal kitchen and bedroom.

The kitchen looks out onto the main road so we get to notice a lot of what is happening. Lynne calls me the Neighbourhood Watcher. Totally uncalled for, although, to be fair, I do have a pair of binoculars handy to supplement my failing eyesight.

I find it totally unfair that Nature lets you remain forever young in your head but systematically downgrades everything else.

I, who used to have hawk-like vision, now have to resort to glasses.

My hearing, which used to be superb, is now reduced to deciphering the outside world through what feels like cotton wool stuffed ears. As Lynne, who is three years younger than me, constantly shouts from her room to mine, I might indeed need to get them checked.

And why, whilst on the subject, does Nature insist that you automatically groan as you get in and out of chairs?

Slowly thins out the hair on your head but, to compensate, induces your nose and ears to start growing copious amounts of a black and wiry equivalent for public display?

Let you get down on your knees but fails to provide sufficient suppleness or energy to get back up?

Or make you shuffle about the house instead of your once confident striding? Make you prefer carpet slippers to shoes. Make you groan as you slowly climb the stairs and rest, panting and perspiring, on the landing?

A very old guy, on reflection he was about my age, once told me that 'Death is Nature's way of telling you to slow down'.

Maybe he had a point. He slowed right down about four years ago. I attended his funeral.

As you get older you seem to attend many funerals. And the most interesting part of the local paper seems to be the Obituary section.

You read that old So and So has gone to collect the Pension in the Sky. Sadly the news doesn't sadden you. You even get a perverse satisfaction in having outlived him.

But, I am now getting morbid. Getting old does that to you. In fact.........no, stop this right now. Sixty seven (and a quarter) is not old. It's the new Forty. Get a grip man. Stop moaning. You sound like a miserable old git.

Having spent a lot of years driving on the continent, I find that the foreigners do some things ok. The Germans make good food. The Italians gave us pasta. The French give us grief. The Spanish are best of all. They gave me the siesta.

Most afternoons I stagger upstairs, five dogs in tow, and lay on the bed. I don't have much choice as the dogs know my system too well and start barking as soon as I say "Ah, well….."

Unless I'm really lucky, I don't sleep. I just lay there, unmoving and close my eyes for an hour or so.

But, that is enough. I get up suitably refreshed and ready to take on the rest of the day. Indulgent? Yeah but, by mid-day, I have usually been up for six or seven hours.

Another one of Nature's foibles. Because you have so much time on your hands when you retire, filling in your day can be a problem. Hence the allotment.

But Nature makes it even harder by short changing you on sleep. Making the days even longer. I go to bed at eleven. Watch Family Guy for twenty minutes or so then go to sleep.

No problem going to sleep. I'm out like a light then wide awake again in three hours or so. Come half four-ish, after an hour of trying to get back to sleep, I usually get up.

I remember fondly the great nights of deep sleep I had in my sleeper cab. That unconscious, dead to the world, sort of sleep. Usually after a very long day's driving.

All that deep sleep stopped when I retired from the road. I once tried to replicate the conditions in my cab by installing a truck engine under the bed but the Boss complained about the dirt and diesel smell.

I pointed out that she had given me a bottle of Diesel deodorant for Christmas. Actually, I'm still not too sure about that deodorant.

I still have the sneaky suspicion it came straight from the pump.

May be the cough mixture bottle was the giveaway? – Also, I reminded her, she had years of being with me, my dirt and my diesel smell. She still wasn't amused.

A cup of tea when I get up and then the rest of the day to look forward to. What do I do? I write of course. Silly question. I'm currently writing about a bunch of old fogeys and their antics on an allotment. I hope it catches on.

So, come mid-day, I am ready for a nap. Getting old sucks sometimes. But, at least you get a free Bus Pass.

So, between a hectic home life and a needy allotment, I manage to fill in my days.

All of which reminds me. The 'I'll get back to that later' list.

Perhaps now is as good a time as ever to tell the story of what happened on the allotment last year.

It is a story of how The Allotmenteers came into being in a desperate fight against evil. How good prevailed. The reasons and the consequences.

A tale of heroics and daring and......sorry, damn computer slipped into BS mode again.

What, you don't have a BS button on your keyboard? No, on reflection, you wouldn't.

The special BS button keyboards are reserved for special people. You have to be a politician, a banker, a lawyer or a journalist to have one.

Chapter Five.

The Victory Allotment wasn't always the haven of peace, quiet and getting out of the house, it is today.

Up until last year, there was a lot of unrest, destruction, arson and bullying. The plot turnover on the bottom plots was high.

Tenants were scared to talk to each other for fear of reprisals. There was blackmail and extortion. And one man was responsible: Albert 'Bert' Collins.

Collins was around average height with the ruddy face and broken veins of a heavy drinker. On a good day he looked like Jack Nickolson with extra wrinkles. A lot of extra wrinkles. On a good day he could turn milk into yogurt by staring at it.

His receding hair was firmly brushed forward from the neck into a Roman style fringe. Although, unless he removed his habitual base ball cap, you couldn't see his hair.

He had a very distinctive rolling walk. From the front he looked slim but, viewed from the side, the reason for this curious walk was revealed. A large protruding stomach had to be compensated for by a very stiff back and a wide leg stance.

Whether from drink or a glandular problem, the reason for the heavily pregnant look wasn't known. He compensated for it by his curious walk and by balancing a large chip of resentment on his shoulders.

Collins had arrived from another allotment in nearby Dunchurch. Here, the allotment committee, fed up with his bad attitude, had given him notice to quit.

 Additionally, the committee of this privately run allotment had reinforced its decision by dumping his tools and disassembled shed outside the allotment gates.

A new, very large, padlock confirmed there would be no appeal of any kind.

From there, he had arrived at the Victory Allotments. Because he knew that John Burns, the manager of the Parks and Open Spaces office was having an affair, he used this knowledge to get a plot and safeguard his tenancy of that plot.

Within a year, he had extended to a separate adjacent plot. There was a shed on each plot and, give him his due, both were in excellent shape.

After the humiliation of the Dunchurch allotments, Collins set about making sure the same thing didn't happen again.

Apart from having Burns on his side, he wanted to get some sort of committee going and become in charge of that.

To every newcomer he appeared to be friendly, helpful and an all round nice guy. But let anyone fail to keep his plot in shape and Collins was soon there to show the tenant the error of his ways. Mr Nice very quickly became Mr nasty.

A friendly word of warning, if ignored, quickly became more forceful. Then the sabotage would begin if the condition of the plot, and enthusiasm of the tenant, didn't quickly improve.

Crops would die because of the weed killer sprayed on them. The threats would become physical and, if that didn't work, a shed would mysteriously burn down overnight.

Because of the layout of the allotment, most of this took place on the bottom plots.

The top plots were usually taken by long term tenants. Generally older they had more time to keep their plots in shape and, as they were all friends, more united in stopping Collins' crusade.

What we didn't know at the time was that there was another, more sinister, reason for Collins wanting to ensure the allotments continued and flourished.

One persistent rumour making the rounds was that the council were more interested in selling the allotment as building land than keeping would-be allotmenteers happy.

Collins' plan to thwart this was to make sure the plots were kept in good shape and occupied.

The more tenants, the harder it would be for the council to find under tenancy as an excuse for getting rid of a no- profit problem and gaining a lot of extra money as a bonus.

But, the constant friction and war on nerves meant that the Victory Allotments were not a happy place to be.

I first met Collins when I was being shown around the allotments by Geoffrey Leighton-Bradbury. Geoff was the guy I met in Aldi who told me about his allotment and how to get round the council waiting list.

He wasn't really interested in his plot for the usual reasons. Growing vegetables and the work it entailed wasn't for him.

He got the plot because it gave him an excuse to meet up with his girlfriend Jane who just happened to be his house gardner.

Collins had happened upon him planting his carrot seed with Jane in the comfort of his large shed and single bed.

 He had then decided that £50 a week was a suitable sum for keeping quiet. Geoff was a deputy bank manager so the money wasn't that much of a problem for him. He paid up.

We were on his plot and he was telling me how to get round the council waiting list.

This simply involved the tenant informing the council that he was taking on a co-worker. The arrangement of labour and produce division was left to the tenant and his co-worker.

But, and this was the key, if the tenant decided to leave the co-worker would automatically be given the option of taking on the plot for himself.

The plan for me was that I would approach Old Albert, an elderly tenant, and become his co-worker. Geoff felt that Old Albert would be more than amenable to such a proposal.

Collins showed up as this conversation was taking place. Ignoring me completely, he loudly demanded his weekly hush money from Geoff.

Geoff had forgotten to bring it in the excitement of having someone to show off his allotment to.

Despite his attempts to explain that he would bring it the next day, Collins moved in, grabbed him by his cravat –Geoff always dressed nice even for the allotment – pulled him halfway over the fence and proceed to throttle him.

I stepped in and it ended up with Collins on his knees in front of me. I might look old and decrepit but I am also very strong. I should also mention that I have a temper. Normally I keep this under control but I have always hated bullies.

Collins found that out when I got him on the ground and proceed to kick him until he asked me to stop.

"I say, old boy, would you mind stopping that right now? I'm getting most frightfully sore." Or something similar.

The upshot was that I made both a friend and an enemy in one day.

Geoff was so surprised and grateful that he decided a good insurance policy for him would be for me to be his co-worker.

Collins, once out of earshot, swore vengeance for his humiliation and the less than fond memories of Dunchurch it bought rushing back to him.

He ignored me after that but the news of his downfall very quickly became public allotment knowledge.

Adrian's house overlooks the allotments and he witnessed the whole thing from his kitchen window.

He discussed it with his plot neighbours and the upshot was that a deputation of four turned up at my house one morning for a chat. Lynne led them up the garden path to where I was resting my eyes in my large workshop.

It was afterwards that Lynne suddenly decided she loved Adrian's white hair. Even to the point of asking me why I didn't have white hair.

I too sometimes wondered why my hair wasn't snow white. She certainly gives me enough grief to warrant it turning completely snow white overnight.

That workshop chat became the start of the concerted effort to get rid of Collins. It also became the reason why four old guys and one younger one became the Allotmenteers. All for One and One for All and All That. But not Take That. They weren't invited.

When you got a problem… who you gonna call? Big Mick, Paul, Pete, Adrian and Dave.

We began an all out effort to humiliate him. We dressed in similar clothes to him and marched around the allotments with his distinctive rolling walk. The other allotmenteers howled with laughter. Collins just glowered and simmered

Geoff's shed got burnt down one night in retaliation for that little exercise.

Things hotted up. Pete used his locksmith skills to pick the fuel filler cap on Collins' van. He poured a gallon of red, home heating oil/diesel into the tank and then informed Customs and Excise that Collins was using untaxed diesel in his vehicle.

 Customs and Excise turned up at his house, did a diesel test and charged him.

 Around the same time, a lot of speeding tickets from speed camera generated offences began arriving almost daily.

That was down to me. I borrowed an identical van to the one Collins drove from a car breaker friend of mine. The same friend also supplied a set of registration plates with the number of Collins' van on them.

I then drove around the area and got caught on as many speed cameras as I could. I wore a baseball cap pulled down low. This not only concealed my identity but made it look as if Collins was the driver.

We also painted his two sheds a shocking shade of pink. This was after an Allotmenteers meeting at a pub. It seemed a good idea at the time.

When Collins arrived at the allotments the next morning he was already in a bad mood. More speeding tickets had arrived in the post.

Seeing the pink sheds and hearing all the laughter, he snapped. He lashed out at the nearest person, punched him to the ground and proceeded to kick him enthusiastically.

This proved to much for the other plot holders. They united as a team and grabbed Collins. They then began to unleash all the resentment, fear and loathing they had accumulated as his victims. They began to beat the crap out of him.

Much against out instincts, the Allotmenteers stepped in and rescued him. We got him to his van and told him to go while he still could. We never saw him again.

The council, and John Burns in particular, were very happy to see him go. Not that they had a choice after the wife of Collins' victim turned up threatening a law suit if they didn't get rid of him.

We later found out that he had left the area. Just walked out of his council house leaving a pile of speeding tickets and a court summons for the red diesel offence.

He withdrew all his money from the bank, exchanged his van for a camper van and took the Eurostar train to France. There had been no news about him since.

Not that we were looking for him. It was the police and Interpol who were looking.

Some time after he vacated his plot, the council sent in workers to remove the offensive pink sheds and rotovate the plots.

I was there when the rotovator turned up the body of a young Polish lady who had been buried under the larger of the two sheds.

Kinga Sadlek had been Collins' live in girlfriend. Evidence from neighbours and former girlfriends confirmed that Collins liked to use his fists on women.

Although the post mortem evidence showed that the Hyroid bone had been broken, a mark of strangulation, it also revealed that Kinga had been the victim of regular beatings resulting in breaks and fractures.

It was widely assumed that the reason for Collins not wanting the allotments broken up or sold was so the body was not found in his lifetime.

Jan Hawk'nspit, the shop keeper, had known Kinga and had often pleaded with her to leave Collins. When she dropped out of circulation, he and everyone who knew her, assumed she had come to her senses and left the area.

The whole episode was a mix of delight and sadness. Whole hearted delight that Collins had gone. Sadness that the body of a young woman had been found.

We, as the Allotmenteers, had the same mixed reactions. Things hadn't turned out quite as we expected. We had the end result we wanted but it wasn't as gratifying as we had anticipated.

The only positive thing to come out of it was the discovery of Kinga Sadlek. Not that it was a good thing but at least her mother, who lived down in Kent, now knew what had happened to the daughter who had run away from home.

She took the remains back to Poland and Kinga was buried in the family plot.

The council didn't quite know what to do with Collins' two plots. In the end, it decided to off load the problem by letting the tenants of the Victory Allotments make the decision.

We had a meeting. The others passed the problem onto the Allotmenteers. The five of us took very little time to decide. We passed our suggestion back to the larger group. The vote was unanimous.

We all chipped in with time, supplies, money and labour.

We put a white picket fence around the plots. We planted flowers around the fence. The whole area was turfed. We designed and built a three sided shelter that looked out onto the allotments. We put rechargeable lights, powered by a solar panel, inside.

We put a plaque of remembrance on one of the walls.

It became an area of quiet and contemplation. Kinga's mother and several relatives visited. They thanked us for our kindness in creating an English memorial to her.

We made it nice and we kept it nice. It was a joint effort. It brought us all together as a team and not just as a mixed bag of plot holders.

It serves to remind people not to forget Kinga. It keeps her in our memory.

Kinga's mother, Anya, comes up from Kent regularly. She sits inside to pray and remember her daughter. She says it brings her great comfort.

An assortment of Rugby's Polish population come and visit as well. They are respectful, polite and grateful that we have done this for one of their own.

In her own tragic way, Kinga Sadlek has reached out and brought two nations together in compassion and understanding.

There is even talk of renaming the allotments in her memory.

That was last year. A troubled time for the Victory Allotments. A time we hope to put behind us but can never quite forget.

Chapter Six

The next morning was one of those freak late February days. It had been warm the day before and the weather girl was forecasting an even hotter prolonged spell.

This was the BBC weather girl so it had to be accurate. I have noticed that the commercial weather reports are less so. And don't even get me started on the state of the weather since the Conservatives got in. Its never been the same since.

So far, it had been a mild winter. Dark and dismal but only a flurry of snow, a few sharp frosts, a few days of rain and the occasional gale. About normal for Hillmorton. The rest of the country....well that was another matter.

Because today was a Saturday, I expected record crowds down the allotment. We tend to get a lot of week-end weeders due to work commitments during the week.

There were only a few vacant plots left. We had an influx of immigrant workers taking up a plot. One or two were seen to be building little houses but a quick word to Parks and Open Spaces manager, John Burns, put a stop to that.

Since Collins had moved on, John Burns and I get on well. He had ended his affair and made up with his wife. He told me in confidence that the council were no longer pursuing selling the allotments for housing.

A combination of boggy ground and the proximity of the Great Western rail line had been enough for the rethink.

John's main role now was to keep us happy. He was lazy but also clever enough to realise that we could police our own allotments with very little interference.

After what had happened with Collins, the tenants were resolved that the same situation wouldn't happen again.

There wasn't an official committee but some of the older top and bottom plot guys were seen as referees in sorting out disputes, making sure plots were looked after and making sure everyone was treated equally.

Start to make trouble and there was one warning. Ignore it and there was an all tenant meeting and vote to either resolve the problem or end it.

In effect we governed ourselves and it worked. The Victory Allotment was a much happier place than it had been.

People worked together, helped each other and took a pride in their plots in particular and the Victory Allotment in general.

Of course there was still the hierarchy of Top and Bottom. Nothing could be done about that. But, if nothing else, it gave the common Botom people something to aspire to.

So, as I walked down the road that morning, I was content with the way things had worked out. I had a five minute walk before I reached the Bottom gate.

This was the same as the Top gate but without the car park. Two galvanised gates with wire mesh enclosures and a good padlock. The chain link fence that ran around the boundaries of the allotment were attached to either end.

I opened them, walked through and closed them after me. The path led through a little spinney of straggly trees. They were spindly but tall enough to create a tunnel effect. There was the sound of running water to my left.

On my first visit here I had thought it to be a brook. It would have completed the picture: a babbling, sparkling brook with fish swimming lazily around. In reality it was an open drain that dealt with the run off from the nearby road.

I walked towards the light. There was no Heavenly Choir but, at the end of the dark spinney tunnel, there was a sight I had come to appreciate every time I saw it.

The path opened out into the allotments. Allotments to the left of me. Allotments to the right of me.

All of them fenced off with some sort of barrier. Some had chain link fencing, others had wooden picket fences, others just a ramshackle collection of broken pallets, splinters of wood, hope and optimism.

Some stood forlornly in untouched winter desolation. Others showed the first signs of recent tending. A row of dug earth. A patch of cleared ground.

Within a few weeks most would be cleared, dug and planted.

A few, very few, were kept as gardens. They were turfed, tended and treasured by the occupants of gardenless homes and flats.

In the summer you could see these occupants sitting in their chairs, shed door open and light music relaxing them. Content to have a little bit of green to call their own. And all for the bargain price of £30 a year.

A space to escape their rowing neighbours, barking dogs and the pressure cooker of too many people living too close to each other.

These Shangri La's had little nameplates with Welcome to my Garden, My Repose and similar wistful names hung on their fences.

There would be a grumbling of goblins, a deputation of dwarves or a flight of fairies scattered amongst the flowers and the little rockeries. Little spades, forks and wheelbarrows brightly proclaimed the presence of young children or grandchildren.

You would see barbecues on the week-end when all the allotment neighbours, near and far, were invited.

You would see young and old mixing, enjoying themselves, helping each other, swopping seeds, tips, tools and advice.

You would see the real magic of an allotment. The magic that transcended fresh vegetables, healthy exercise and the siren call of tv gardening programmes.

You would see people's smiles and have a contented smile of your own.

Or you could have an allotment just to escape the wife.

I used to have that luxury. But, last summer, Lynne had decided to visit. She looked at my new shed, admired my raised beds –just like Alan would build them – and saw the possibilities. When Adrian came over and flaunted his white hair in her face, she was instantly smitten.

Within a few days she had moved in. My oasis of a shed became a hoard of easels, paints and paint brushes. My easy life became a series of tasks dictated by The Boss as she sat outside in comfortable splendor.

She painted, pointed, planned and, sometimes, pottered. Thoughts of going back to truck driving began to dominate my waking thoughts.

Thoughts that quickly died as the cold light of realism sank in. I was too old, too tired and too settled to go gallivanting across europe yet again.

Getting old sucks sometimes. Naw, getting old sucks most of the time.

But, this morning, as I made my way to OUR shed, I was content. A cuppa, a relax and maybe a bit of digging.

I had dug my potato patch last autumn in order to allow the winter ravages to break the soil up. All I had to do now was ridge it up, plant my spuds and re-ridged it over them.

I was looking forward to a little solitude. A little ME time. Then I saw Adrian and a woman standing in his plot and looking in my direction.

Chapter Seven.

As I got closer I realised the woman was Kinga Sadlek's mother, Anya. She was a late fifty-ish woman. I have never been brave enough to accurately guess a woman's age.

Suffice to say she was leaning towards being plump boned with auburn hair and an engaging face. Her smile and big baby blue eyes were her best features.

She had been coming up as lot lately to spend time in our memorial area. She said it helped her. I noticed that she liked looking at Adrian. That white hair again.

"Hello Anya, how are you?" I asked as we shook hands continental style. She looked a lot better than the grief stricken woman I first saw last year.

"Yes, I am well, zank you." She said in her good but accented English. I remember Adrian telling me that she had been an English teacher in Poland. That she had come to England in the 80's to teach German, met her husband and stayed. She lived in Kent and had lost her husband to cancer in 2001.

 Looking at Adrian and her together, it suddenly struck me that Adrian had told me a lot about her. Something going on?

"Anya has a problem with her car." Adrian told me. "It keeps cutting out. She was lucky to get here.

She was going to call out the AA but found her membership had lapsed last month. I called Paul out and he is looking at it now.

I brought Anya up here to get her a cup of tea when we saw you coming. Would you like to join us?"

Old White Head was standing just behind her and slowly shaking his old white head. I got the message.

"Naw, it's all right , mate." I assured him. "I've just had one. You go ahead. I'll let you know when Paul has finished." He turned to lead Anya away and I gave him a quick wink. He coloured slightly.

I got my little Mantis tiller out of the shed and began to turn the earth on my spud patch. It didn't take much to get a good tilth going – I am learning to speak technical Allotmentese – and I was soon finished.

I attached the handy little furrowing plough and created several reasonably straight ridges. I returned to the shed for my early Arran Pilot seed potatoes. These had been chitting – a technical term meaning sprouting tubers – for a couple of weeks in the coal shed at home.

I planted one every foot or so apart until all forty were in the ground. I started up the Mantis and reverse-ridged the furrows to cover the potatoes. Stand back, watch and pick lovely new potatoes in about 5-6 weeks. Easy peasy.

"Planting them early, aren't you?" Paul asked. He had come up unnoticed behind me. I reminded myself to book a hearing appointment with SpecSavers when next in town. I looked at him.

"Yeah, well, get them in while the weather is good. Once they're planted and covered they're safe from late frosts. The early bird gets the new potatoes first."

There was also a competitive edge to getting the new spuds in first. Some of the guys used to come down really early in the morning or late evenings to get the ground prepared and planted in secret.

Paul tends to dress like me. Charity Boutique chic. Jeans, tee shirt and 'not bothered about getting it dirty' coat. His hands were black and I guess he was after some of the hand cleaner I had inside my shed.

One of the perks of being a transport journalist, retired or not, was that companies kept sending me stuff to test. I used to ring them up and remind them I was now retired but it was somehow easier to keep sending me test stuff than take my name off a list.

Hence the hand cleaner called Working Hands which did what it said on the lid.

After he had cleaned up, I brewed us both a cuppa. Adrian had seen us and he and Anya joined us. Adrian asked Paul if he had fixed the car.

Paul has always been a bit quiet, bashful or plain taciturn so he just nodded his head. Anya asked him what the problem was and how much she owed him.

"It is fine now and you don't owe me anything." He told her.

"Well, zank you. But, what was the problem in case if happens again? Is there anything I can do to fix it?"

Paul removed his cap, mopped his head with a large non too clean handkerchief and replaced his headgear. He looked funny without it. "Crap in the fuel filter." He finally volunteered.

Anya looked at him a bit puzzled. "How often must I do that?" she asked. Then looked even more puzzled as Adrian and I burst out laughing. Even Paul very nearly cracked a little smile.

We sat around drinking out tea and talking. Paul kept looking at his hands and then smelling them. "That hand cream is really good." He said. "Where did you get it from?"

That led into a discussion about my journalistic days. The press do's and foreign travel. The posh hotels and long hours. They listened enviously as I told them I had even travelled on the Orient Express with a full English and Bucks Fizz for breakfast.

I told them of all the vehicles I had to test. The long road development tests I had done. They seemed interested and I tried not to make it look like I was boasting.

I knew I was lucky. An eye infection had stopped me driving trucks for a while. In one of those in creditably lucky chances that come along, I had wandered into transport journalism. I had been good at it and lucky.

Many of my journalist colleagues, a bit resentful of my success, told me I was lucky.

I agreed with them that I was lucky.

Also I remarked, the strange thing was, the harder I worked, the luckier I seemed to get.

Adrian asked me if I had any experience with hybrid or electrical vehicles. He said he was considering buying a Toyota Prius and wanted some advice. I told him it was, in my estimate, a good car. I am very pro-Japanese vehicles anyway.

I also told him that I had once driven an all electric development car from Land's End to John O' Groats. "It wasn't that fast on the motorway." I told him. "But it was comfortable." He asked about economy.

"The economy was great. We totted up the costs after the test had been completed. The cost of driving from one end of the country to the other came to £7. 83 pence."

"Bloody hell" Adrian exclaimed. "That sounds like my type of car. What make is it and when is it coming out?"

"The sad fact is that it isn't going into production." I told him. "The manufacturer belatedly found a really bad flaw in its projected cost calculations."

"Oh." Adrian looked disappointed. "What was the problem?"

"They found out that the cost of the cable came to £34,102.10." I told him with a straight face.

He got there eventually.

"Yes, very funny I'm sure. You got me there." He admitted as he tried to stifle a laugh. "Good one."

Paul got up to go. He said his goodbyes, walked off then returned. "Anyone fancy a night at the Red Lion?" he asked.

Did we? Suddenly a night out at the Red Lion seemed like a very good idea. Adrian said he would ring the rest of the Allotmenteers. Usual time, usual place.

One for All and All for One. But…you buy your own drinks.

Chapter Eight.

Jan Hawk'nspit left his wife in charge of the shop and went to see his friend and competitor at the Indian shop.

Ramanan Balakrishnan, like Jan, had also been renamed by the shopping community. To all of his customers he was known simply as Jimmy.

He and his Polish friend shared both a profession and a problem. "Those bollocking kids" as Jan called them.

Both were losing goods and customers to the gang that seemed to be permanently around their shops. Not to mention the litter, the swearing, customer intimidation and general anti-social behaviour.

Bad enough during school term but rapidly escalating during the seemingly over-long holidays.

Particularly the endless summer days and long evenings.

The police would be called but, at the first signs of their arrival, the gang would be gone.

Back down to the recreation park to plot their next move and sullenly wait for the police to go. Then back to the shops. It was a routine that was both predictable and unwelcome.

But, after throwing ideas around, many impractical and others downright illegal, the two shop keepers were no nearer a solution.

Finally Jan decided he would talk it over with a few people he knew down the allotment. The rumour was that they had been very effective at dealing with an allotment problem. Very effective indeed.

Just as he was leaving Jimmy's shop he heard his wife's angry shouting in Polish. He looked towards the end of the parade and saw a group of youths running from his own shop.

He also saw that most of them were carrying packets of crisps, bottles of pop and similar 'grab quick and run' items of his stock.

He had the illogical thought and momentary flash of pride that the local youths were developing a taste for his Polish imported goods. If he could only get them to pay for them, he would be content.

His wife was in tears. Jan looked at the departing kids and swore that something had to be, was going to be, done about those bollocking kids.

He knew just who he was going to talk to.

Chapter Nine.

The M1 motorway started from Junction 5, Watford, in November 1959 and ended at Junction 18 Rugby/Crick.

The Red Lion pub in Crick is on the main road through the village. Prior to the motorway Crick was a typical sleepy English hamlet. The motorway changed all that.

Following the motorway and its fast transportation links came progress. Progress in the shape of new businesses, labour requirements and housing.

The continuation of the M1 towards Leeds in 1965 and the start of the nearby M6 –Rugby is Junction 1 of the M6 – around the same time increased those needs.

New warehouses began to appear, almost overnight, on former farm land next to the motorway monster. Farmers became rich overnight when they sold the land that had been in the family for centuries.

In the 1990's the Daventry International Rail Freight terminal, D.I.R.F.T, created thousands more jobs.

Crick went from a sleepy village to a large village. New houses were built to meet ever increasing need. And, not just at Crick.

The nearest town is Rugby and that has virtually quadrupled over the decades since vehicles first started on the new adventures and love affairs of and with motorways.

There is now talk of building homes on the site of the former Radio Masts of Rugby. Those towering iron landmarks that, for decades, proudly served to tell Rugby folk that they are home.

Now those once welcoming masts are replaced by several of those monstrous white windmills. There to generate electricity - but rarely seen turning - and be universally hated and loathed by the passing motorway traffic.

The same motorways that gave us easy access to faraway destinations. To the myriad delights of motorway services and the large car parks they have since become.

My grandkids think I'm joking when I tell them that, in the early days, motorists used to drive up the motorways to have a good meal at the nearest service area. Then they had waitress service, exciting new foods and convivial atmospheres.

The traffic on motorways used to be able to speed along all day with no hold-ups or roadwork's. Hasn't changed much, has it?

Anyway, back to Crick. It coped with the new and exciting challenges. Sort of. The little main road began to deteriorate under the sheer numbers of vehicles passing through. Old people used to line up like lemmings to cross the road.

People began to complain and oppose new developments. Eventually, a little while ago, a new bypass was built.

Almost overnight, the village became a vehicular desert. People could walk around without breathing carbon monoxide cocktails.

Children could once again walk safely to school. Inebriated men could once again doze by the side of the road without falling prey to the thumping tyres of foreign juggernauts.

The old timers could take all the time they wanted, or had left, to cross the main road.

Progress had been halted. Crick began to slew off its modernity and revert to the old ways, the good old ways.

It became once again a sleepy jewel concealed in the leafy lanes and whimsical roads of a forgotten era.

A safe haven for the memories of the never forgotten heroes of WW2. A fitting memorial for those who gave their lives in far flung, forgotten shores, never again to return to their roots and grieving loved ones.

Where little Johnny could sleep safely in his own little bed each night.

Where the WI still meet to make rhubarb jam, scones and to sing Jerusalem.

Where the village blacksmith still toiled under his spreading chestnut tree, making horseshoes for the sole representative of this slumbering one horse village.

This pearl in this green and pleasant land. This................

Sorry, back again. Just had to pop into town to deposit my cheque from the Crick tourist board. Now, where was I?..Oh yeah.

The Red Lion. That quintessential example of a traditional English public house. The meeting place of the village and safe refuge from marauding wives and girlfriends.

Where men were men and women were glad of them. Where........Bloody computer. Stuck in BS mode again!

I drove into the car park and was closely followed by Adrian and Mick in Old White Head's car. Big Mick's tatty Transit van was already parked.

The car park wasn't very big and more suited to its designed horse and cart traffic.

Inside it kept its traditional look and feel. There were low ceilings with black beams time-etched and transformed by years of tobacco smoke, short cleaners and the hair products of increasingly taller men.

The traditional bar was central and manned by a traditional landlord of good cheer and bon homie. Brass tankards and horse brasses winked in the reflection of the seemingly permanent wood fire. The wooden benches alongside the wall were polished to a sheen by countless bottoms.

The soft bar stools forever shaped by the bodies of the locals who claimed them as their own. And woe betide anyone else who had the audacity to sit on them.

As we entered, all conversation stopped. Suspicious eyes looked at us from under shaggy fringes, huge bushy eyebrows and moth eaten caps. The old timers, playing their endless game with matches and drilled planks of wood, collectively looked up with the hope of a free drink.

Finally, we were recognised, greeted and allowed to approach the bar. We ordered our drinks from the now amiable dispenser of good cheer, fatigue numbing and thirst quenching alcoholic beverages.

We spotted Big Mick in the far corner. He looked as if he had already sampled several of the aforementioned beverages.

He stood up to indicate where he was. Picked up the table he had knocked down and sank, nay collapsed, into his seat. We joined him.

He had the slightly cross eyed, red face and beery breath of a habitual drunkard. But, a couple more and he would be sober again.

It was almost as if he imbibed the alcohol and then instantly shed it from his sweat pores. It was a phenomomen we had seen time and time again. It would have been impressive if not for the soaking wet clothes and ripe odour.

But, we had all watched CSI, Body of Proof and similar shows. We knew the score. A dab of Vicks under each nostril and the wearer of this magic potion was immune to smell.

A few of the locals gurned at us. We waved back. It had taken almost a year of coming here on a regular basis to be reluctantly accepted. It was a humbling experience for us men of the outside world to be taken into the inner circle of these shy and secretive people.

We had chosen our clothing with care. Sensitive to our surroundings and wishing to blend in.

We had dressed casual. Un-ironed and rumpled tee shirts, baggy trousers secured mid calf with baling twine – to stop rodents entering - and old but comfortable footwear.

Disguises secured by many forays into the hidden depths of the myriad of charity shops that grace Rugby with their presence.

Clothing items bought with scant regard for the latest fashion. In styles and materials that would, once every decade or so, propel us protesting loudly into the very pinnacles of up to date peacock shaming modernity.

Lynne reckoned we dressed like slobs. I called it comfortably casual.

So we sat and drank. Beers with patriotic names like Old Growler, Thunder Pants and Old Slag Stout. Lagers from continental climes. Lemonade, for me, from the fine cellars of R Whites. This ambrosial drink cunningly coloured with just a hint of lager to resemble a real man's drink.

Enough to disguise the fact that I am a secret lemonade drinker.

Big Mick regaled the whole pub with his increasingly risqué jokes. I'll give you the cleanest and stop there before I have to go into a much higher readership age bracket.

".....So they are coming back from the pub and one of them stops to milk the python. He is standing there pressure washing the ancient dry stone walling when his mate climbs over a gate.

Next second he is staggering wildly across the field towards a flock of sheep.

He dives in and somehow manages to catch one. He is dragging it back towards the gate when the one beside the now clean but collapsed wall shouts out to him "Are you going to shear that sheep?"

His mate calls back breathlessly. "No. Get your bloody own."

Over in the corner, the old men look up. They smile their toothless smiles and cackle their laughter. Old memories, fond memories, of the woolly-haired passions of youth again rekindled. They point at us and give shaky high sixes to each other.

For no particular reason, one pitifully raises himself off his stool, stands as upright as his shaking legs and stooped shoulders allow and bursts in song.   His friends begin to shuush everyone.

"There'll be blue birds over the white cliffs of Dover....." he sings in a surprisingly good baritone voice.

One by one the others slowly stand and join in. Softly at first and then with increasing strength and volume.

A veritable choir of The Ancients. Voices from the past. The sound pulled and tugged on our senses. The hairs on the back of my neck stand up. All noise in the pub stops. Everyone is silent, listening and appreciating.

On the second verse, a few drop out. Then a few more and then only the original one is left standing. He looks around with tears streaming down his face. Looks at his mates, shakes his head and stops mid verse. Sits slowly and wearily down.

We hear one of the nearby locals telling his companion. "Never fails. They get going, are doing well, then one by one, they forget the bloody words."

To break the silence, Big Mick turns to me. "You used to go to Dover, didn't you?" he asks with his very fruity breath wafting over me. I hold my breath, dab at my streaming eyes and nod my head.

"Are the cliffs really white?" I nod my head. "Why are they white?" he asks.

I once spent a coach engine development fortnight with an Australian. He drove his own coach round the test route and I drove an identical one but with the new engine fitted.

Every night at the hotel he would regale us with tales from his job, life experiences, Sheila's and Oz. In the UK his job involved taking our American cousins on coach tours to see the castles, sights and wonders of our 'little ol' country.

One of his group once asked him why the cliffs of Dover were white. I liked this Aussie guy because his weird sense of humour was similar to mine.

"During WW2" he told his engrossed audience "there were many aerial dogfights over the English channel. German and English pilots would fight it out in spectacular aerial combat.

The problem was that, with all the maneuvers, body rolls and the like, the pilots would quickly become disorientated.

There was no way of distinguishing the brown cliffs of England to the very similar brown cliffs of France.

Obviously the English pilots wanted to land in England and the Germans in France. But both sides kept getting mixed up and landing in the wrong country.

So the War Committee thought about the problem and arrived at a pretty spectacular solution. Basically they got a lot of volunteers, together with a lot of brushes and whitewash, and they painted the brown cliffs of Dover white.

After that, no pilot ever got confused again. They have kept the cliffs white since then, as a mark of remembrance and just in case they were ever needed again."

There was a silence then a smattering of applause from his coach bound Americans.

Then one turned to his friend and said "Doggone it, you gotta hand it to these Limeys. What an elegantly simple solution to a big problem."

Many, many trips and tips later, he was still telling that story. And they were still believing him.

It makes the old joke about McDonalds almost believable. Seventeen per cent of all Americans have worked for McDonalds, so the joke goes. The punchline is that the others weren't clever enough.

I told Big Mick why the cliffs of Dover were white. He thought about it. Turned to Pete. "I knew he'd know. He's a clever bugger is our Dave. Must have taken a lot paint though. Now, have you heard the one about the Bishop, the nun and the apple pie?........"

Chapter Ten.

We had chosen the Red Lion for our meeting because it was out of Rugby. We wanted somewhere we could meet without being seen. We met here when we were planning our campaign to get rid of Albert Collins.

It was here where Big Mick decided we should have a name. He asked me for ideas and, with my weird sense of humour, I suggested The Allotmenteers. One for All and All for One.

He loved it and instantly adopted it. And, even though he was pretty drunk at the time, the name sort of stuck.

So we became The Allotmenteers and we plotted as we drank. Well, the others drank and I had my disguised lemonade. As well as a weird sense of humour, I also have a weird sense of taste.

Alcohol of any sort tastes horrible to me. People tell me that, if I persevere, I will get to like it. I can't see the point. So I drink my faux beer and the others pretend not to notice.

It was at the Red Lion that we decided that painting Collins' two sheds bright pink would be a good idea.

Not just any bright pink but the shade that should have come with a health warning and red triangles on the tin. It was a horrendous colour. Guaranteed to blister your eyeballs if you looked at it without protective eyewear.

We left the pub, drove to the allotment and, refreshed by the several packs of lagers we bought before leaving, we painted.

On that occasion even I found that a can or three of lager, on a hot summer evening, could taste reasonably good.

 Could even be considered as an aid to decorating. The results spoke for themselves. Apparently drinking and decorating isn't a good idea.

That was the last time we met at the Red Lion to plot and scheme. We had been back quite a few times since them because we quite enjoyed it. Now it had become almost a weekly ritual.

Having a bunch of mates was all relatively new to me. Truck driving is a solitary occupation and I rarely got the time to socialise. Usually I was too busy trying to catch a ferry, driving long distances to load or unload or sleeping like a dead man in some layby or industrial site.

Since I had retired and got the allotment, I suddenly had friends. And, though I always thought of myself as a loner, I did enjoy our get togethers. Obviously I was growing up.

So, whilst watching Big Mick metamorphis from sober to drunk and back to sober, we talked. About the allotment, the tool co-operative, women, politics, women, diy, car maintenance, women: anything and everything.

Paul enthralled us with his talk about fixing a blown head gasket on a Mondeo.

Peter introduced us to the joys of lock picking and the endless possibilities such a skill could bring.

Adrian engrossed us with stories about accounting and how to save taxes.

I might have mentioned trucking across europe and about becoming a transport journalist.

Then, all to soon, it was nine thirty and we decided to call it an evening. My night out pass was only good until ten. After that, the doors would be locked, bolted and the drawbridge of my Englishman's castle raised.

I did have the sneaky thought that my mate Peter could easily outwit any lock and allow me access. But, having recently run out of Brave pills, I reluctantly decided to forgo the night delights of Crick and return home before curfew.

The thought of my Brave pills, and lack of, meant that I would have to ask for something to eat once welcomed home. Normally, whilst under the Brave influence, I would just barge in and demand, yes demand, that I not only be fed but instantly.

And, because I was under the influence, I could never really remember just why I would wake up so black and blue the next morning. Maybe I fell up the stairs?

Just as I was getting into my mpv my mobile rang. Damn, it must have been accidentally switched on. I have to carry one in case 'I had an accident or something' but I do so reluctantly. Fortunately, they forget to tell me to switch it on.

I see no real need to be constantly in touch and available. I am fairly good with computers but the phone revolution passed me by. I see my kids and grandkids texting each other and think 'why not just walk into the next room and talk?' I read some of the inane remarks on their screens and despair.

I watch my grand kids as they constantly reach for their phones and check their messages. The sad aspect is that they do it and don't realise they have done so. It's a reflex action like breathing or eating.

I watch their dancing thumb as they text in their mysterious phone language. M8 for friend. FYI, TYIA, LOL. I confess to not being completely sure of that last one.

Some say it stands for Laugh Out Loud but if Lots of Love is good enough for David Cameron then that must be right.

I see their little 'smiley' faces assortment and can't see anything to smile about.

The only abbreviations I can be sure about are SWALK, Sealed With A Loving Kiss, and Norwich which stood for, I am reliably informed, Nickers Off Ready When I Get Home.

People used to put them on the back of envelopes. My grandkids don't know what I am talking about.

"Yes, I DO know that knickers starts with a K, Smarty Pants. It's a silent K. Well Korwich wouldn't make sense, would it? Well, just use your imagination. Look that's the end of it, all right? It's Norwich.

Oh, don't go on or you'll get a clip around your ears.....Really?.... Since when?.....A law that says you can't hit kids?....Seriously? Good God, next you'll be telling me you can't send five year olds up a chimney any more. You can't?.... Since when?...Another law? Bloody hell, it's no wonder you kids are so soft. In my day........."

Envelopes? Paper containers that you put letters into.

Letters were squares of organic material that people scratched hieroglyphics onto with ink instruments called a pen or a biro. Ink was a blue, black or red concoction of dyes, soot and wood-ash.

No, please look up hieroglyphics, dyes, soot and wood-ash for yourself. There is a manual word search, spell and correct engine called a Dictionary.

You can find it in something called a Library. No….ask your grandad.

I used to tell my grandkids about this form of pre-email communication. How you put something called a Stamp on the Envelope and then put it into a Post Box and it sometimes got Delivered by someone called a Postman or woman.

They smile indulgently and ask "In the good old days Grumps? Before colour was invented?

When everything was in black and white? When there were only three tv programmes for a couple of hours a day? When your remote was a long stick?

Before the internet when dinosaurs were still around? Come on Grumps, let's get you sat down and comfortable." Kids, they don't know they are born.

God knows what they will tell their grandkids. "In the old days, before media implants in your head, people used to have to manually imput information into things called mobiles, tablets and notebooks. You had to press buttons. It was really hard. You kids, you don't know you are born."

And, what about the long term effects? Future generations will have extended thumbs, gradually lose the use of their legs and think of 'outside and playing' as something to be avoided at all costs.

I got my first Motorola mobile phone in 1988. I was working as a freelance journalist but was also the sole Midlands Office contact for a Surrey based PR company. They decided that mobile phones were the future.

Apparently, over time, the technology advanced a little so I was never asked for the Motorola back. It still works so I still use it.

I appreciate that it might, at nine inches, be considered a tad large. Its reassuring brick shape less than aerodynamic. Compared to the superslim models my grandkids use, its two and a half pound weight might be deemed a little heavy.

And, I suppose, the long aerial is a bit conspicuous. But, it still makes and receives calls and that is its purpose, is it not?

Ok, it makes me appear a bit lopsided and it is a bit of a problem getting it out of my pocket.

But, its solid metal construction and pleasing to hold elongated cube shape more than compensate for a few negative points.

To me it is a thing of beauty. A design classic. And, judging by the envious looks I get whilst using it, so do other people. Youngsters tend to mask their envy and lust for it by laughing as if they didn't care. But I see through their charade.

So, my phone rang and I decide to answer it. Hoping it wasn't someone telling me I might be entitled to compensation.

I'm always up for something for nothing and the fact that 'if they don't win, I won't get charged' can sometimes be a deal clincher. However, they do tend to go on and on and my arm gets tired after holding the phone for a while.

"Finally" says the exasperated tone of my beloved. It took a while to answer because the Motorola had got stuck in my pocket. It is a snug fit and the corners can catch sometimes. As they did now. Nothing a needle and thread won't put right.

"On your way home, can you get some milk? I thought we had enough but it went off. Oh and don't forget your pass expires at ten so don't be late." The line went dead.

"Of course I will get the milk, my little rock bunny. Sorry the other stuff went sour but I have told you about staring at it for too long, haven't I?

No, I don't know how long I'll be before I get home. I'll be there when I get there. If I decide to carry on to a nightclub, then I will do so." By now, I could see the others were watching with open mouths, respect and admiration.

"No, you can't go to bed yet. I'll want something to eat when I do finally get home so you will have to wait up. No, sandwiches won't do. I want something freshly cooked. See you when I see you." I made a show of easing it back into my pocket. "That was the wife." I said airily.

"Respect Bro." said an awed Big Mick.

I called in at Jan's for the milk. I locked up and pushed my way through the crowd of sullen kids. "Watch it Grandad." One of them, it looked to be about five, sneered at kneecap level.

I ignored both the remark and it. Jan was outside with a baseball bat in hand. He waited until I got close then quickly unlocked the door and dragged me in after him.

Inside the shop Jan seemed very pleased to see me.

He took the money for the milk and asked "Are you going to the allotment tomorrow? I really need to talk to you."

"About what?" I asked as I pocketed my change and prepared to run the gauntlet.

He pointed outside. Several of the kids were pressed up against the window. The others were milling aimlessly around in circles making weird noises.

There seemed to be a uniform of sorts. The male of the species had hoodies covering their heads and half mast jeans showing brightly coloured underpants. They wore scruffy trainers with laces trailing behind.

The few females, all looked to be about 12 bodywise but had the hard faces of much older women. They wore skimpy tops, ripped knee jeans or low, beltsized skirts with thongs on display. Over made up little faces and frizzy hair completed their ensemble.

"About those bollocking kids. Foo Kinell, they're doing my nuts in. I talk with you tomorrow. All right, you Plonker?"

I nodded my head in agreement. "Cushty, Bro, cushty." I told him. "Luvely Jubbly."

He opened the door, threw me out and quickly locked it after me. I fought my way through the mob back to my mpv. Beat off those who tried to attach themselves to my legs and got in.

Started the engine and inched out onto the road. Those holding onto my bodywork were thrown clear as I quickly accelerated away.

Bollocking kids.

Chapter Eleven.

I just made my curfew. The red 'closing' light was flashing as I parked up. I could hear the security guy start to loudly ring the handbell. He would walk the gardens warning visitors that Dalyn House would soon be closing.

I have no idea who he is. He just turns up.

My parking space is to the side of our house. Our house is on Victory Drive and the garage, carport and hard standing on Maple Road. It gives us a larger corner plot but can be a nuisance sometimes. We can't see the vehicles from the house so, after a lot of malicious damage, I installed several cctv cameras.

I changed my Toyota Landcruiser last year for a Toyota Regius mpv. I also replaced Lynne's little Daihatsu Grand Move estate car for a Toyota Noah mpv, a smaller version of mine.

The more grandkids we have, the more vehicle space we seem to need. It's expensive being a grandparent.

I can walk round on the roadway from the vehicles or, if in a hurry, across the garden. I guessed that The Boss would be both seeing, and enjoying the sight of, me hurrying on the cctv cameras.

Her little trick is to lock the door just as I am within arms length. But, I have devised a method of fooling her. I simply spray shaving foam on the lens. This sudden snow storm confuses her and gives me the leeway I need. It's a pain cleaning the lens the next morning but better than sleeping in the Toyota.

I was inside before she had gathered her wits enough to try to stop me. "You cut that a bit close." She grumped. "Would you like something to eat?"

"Yes, that would be very nice. Thank you, my precious darling."

"Good, well make me something at the same time, will you?" She said something over her shoulder as she left the kitchen.

"What?"

"Get your ears checked. I asked if you enjoyed yourself?"

Food and concern that I had a nice time? This is going to cost me.

"Yes, thank you. Mainly a chat and a laugh. I only had two shandies."

I don't think she likes seeing me enjoy myself. Why else does she keep her eyes closed just as I am about to c......?

On second thoughts, I'll leave that example for now and think of a more suitable one later.

We had cheese on toast. I volunteered to put up more shelves in her shop. Volunteering in our house is the same as in the army. 'I need a volunteer. You.'

I asked her about the kids up at the shops. She agreed they were a nuisance. She always keeps a pepper spray in her shopping bag in case they picked on her. I didn't think that even they were that stupid.

I watched a bit of telly in my room. She, judging by the swearing, played an on-line game then switched over to her Facethingy or Twatter anti-social networking sites.

I guessed that we weren't that much different from any other couple who had been married for 48 years. We rubbed along. I still have the sneaky thought that, with good behaviour, I could have been out in 25 years.

I let the dogs out in the garden for one last time. I didn't interrupt Lynne. She could go out later. Time for bed. Another exciting day over and a fresh one soon beginning.

*****

When you get old, it is always a good morning if you open your eyes. Going to bed is always a bit of a gamble.

 Are my affairs in order? Is my porn hidden? Is it going to be worthwhile doing any next day planning? But, you get lucky and see in yet another new day.

One day I am going to do the 'how many new days have I seen?' calculations. It'll help pass the time.

Chapter Twelve.

Breakfast for me is two cups of tea and some oat crumble biscuits. When I have finished, I creep back upstairs and look in on Lynne. If she is still asleep I prod her with a long stick and then quickly retreat.

If, or when, she is awake I take her breakfast. Lynne's breakfast is always liquid. She has a Magic Bullet thingy that shreds and juices stuff and the resultant liquid is, apparently, very healthy.

 It doesn't look very healthy. It doesn't smell very healthy. It looks like liquid grass and smells like liquid arse. But, that's just me. What do I know?

By mutual consent, I have taken over the housework.

 The conversation went along the lines of "You've nothing to do, so you ARE going to do the housework from now on." I didn't mind. This was pre-allotment days and finding enough to fill a whole day was always a bit problematic. Now, with my housework and the allotment I can fill both the day and the evenings. Oh joy!

Finally I escaped from the drudgery of my housework and, with a spring in my step, I set off for the allotment.

The unusually warm weather was holding and the allotment was waking up prematurely. As were the workers that tended its needs. I counted at least nine people on their plots as I got to mine.

I hadn't got that much to do really. I had the spuds in. The estate was tidy and shipshape. The kettle was on and the shed warm. I made two cups.

Adrian arrived right on time followed shortly by Jan Hawkn'spit. He preferred coffee. He did ask about biscuits. I reminded him he was a shopkeeper.

We sat and drank and appreciated the morning. Finally Jan brought up the reason for him being there. He looked at Adrian and made that secret man sign of a raised eyebrow. I returned it with the universal short head nod and raised double eyebrows that said 'He's ok'.

"It's those bollocking kids. You saw the problem last night." He began. "Evenings and week-ends, they are there. Always looking for an excuse to shoplift, bother my customers and cause bother to me and the other shops as well."

He doesn't talk as it is written. His accent is pretty thick and his English, although understandable, is a hotpotch of mispronunciations and grammar.

The last not entirely his fault as English grammar is entirely different to that of mainland Europe. One of the problems of being the isolated cul de sac of europe.

Over there, our "I am going to the shops" is along the lines of "To the shops, I am going." The last word always being the verb or action word.

To Jan, constructing a sentence in English was a reversal of his native tongue. I was used to it after years on the continent but I could see Adrian struggling a bit.

"So Jan, what do you want us to do?" I asked him. "Have you tried the police?"

He had. As soon as they arrived, the kids disappeared. Once the police car was up the road, they were back.

"Foo Kinell. No good. Useless. Some of the others" he indicated the allotments "say you and your friends got rid of Collins. Is that right?"

"I wouldn't say we got rid of him exactly." I said thinking fast. A lot, make that most, of the tactics The Allotmenteers used against Collins were illegal. That was something we really didn't want becoming public knowledge.

" We all helped make things difficult for him here. But it was murdering Kinga and her being found under his pink shed that must have eventually made him go." I reminded Jan.

"Yes, but can you help me, and the other shop people, with this bollocking kids problem?" He asked.

I looked at Adrian. He was behind Jan and shaking his head.

"I'll tell you what, Jan. I'll have a talk with some of the other guys and see if they have any ideas. Is that ok for now?"

"Ok, zank you. You are a good man, you Plonker. If you help get rid of kids, I give you good discount in shop, ok? Luvely Jubbly bro"

He finished his coffee and went. I looked at Adrian. "It's a bunch of kids. How hard is it going to be? Sick Big Mick on them and job done." I told him about last night. "They are a problem and it needs sorting" He reluctantly agreed.

He was still dubious. But he was an ex accountant and they are always cautious. That was why The Allotmenters was a good team.

We had Big Mick for violence and dismemberment. Paul for his mechanical skills. Pete for his locksmithing and engineering capabilities. Adrian for his white hair and his voice of caution. Me for my contacts and good looks. Bunch of kids? Piece of cake.

"Well, we can talk about it, I suppose. Any rush? Only I am going down to Kent for a few days?" he said. He didn't elaborate.

I said I'd sound out the others and see what they thought. He finished his tea and went to his allotment. His bungalow backs onto his allotment and he had installed a gate between the two. He began walking home.

I played a hunch. "Give my regards to Anya."
I called after him. He stopped dead then
continued as if he hadn't heard me.

Chapter Thirteen.

Big Mick McAvoy was in his shed. It wasn't much of a shed. This one was the replacement for an earlier one that got burnt down during The Troubles as we referred to it. That one hadn't been much to write home about either.

His current version was built from the various sides of the large wooden crates he had scavenged from work. Three sides, a floor and a roof. He hadn't got round to a door, waterproofing the roof or treating the bare wood sides. But, on the plus side, it was around 8 foot by six foot.

He had installed a substantial chair that looked like a two seater settee when empty but much smaller when he was sitting in it.

He had a few long handled tools leaning against the walls.

Whether they were there because he hadn't installed any tool racks or as support for the sagging walls was unclear. But it was immaterial.

Big Mick seldom used any tools. He seldom grew anything. He bought his vegs from Aldi and pretended he had grown them. Whether his wife believed him or not was not known. But, it kept him out of the house so both of them were content.

Micks favourite pastime was masticating. He would fill his mouth with a portion of a hot Greggs' product and slowly savour it as his jaws methodically worked to demolish it. His current treat was a sausage roll but he had no real preference. So long as it came from Greggs he was happy.

He had tried items from Aldi and even Polish stuff from Jan's shop. They were not the same. Didn't even come close. He was a Greggs man.

He grinned happily as I called out to him. We had found it best to warn him of our approach. If he thought someone was after his food he could get quite protective.

I'm not sure whether his wife knew of his single handed fight to keep Greggs solvent. She cooked him 'healthy' food at home with 'healthy' food he 'produced' down the allotments.

Whether she thought that all vegetables came washed, topped and with barcodes or not, she never mentioned it.

I heard him telling Paul once that 'because he only ate his Greggs stuff on the allotment' it was healthy. His line of thinking being that as the food from the allotment was deemed healthy so food ate in the same place must be equally healthy. Simples.

There was no available sitting place so I stood outside. It was downwind and better. He was busily expelling the last dregs of last night's alcoholic beverages through his soaking wet tee shirt.

I told him of the conversation with Jan. His solution was, as always, brilliantly simple.

"I'll go up there one night and batter them" he said between mouthfuls.

I told him that, although it would probably work, we needed to be a bit more subtle. He looked confused. Whether why we needed to be subtle or by the word itself.

I had a rough plan forming in my head but was not ready to discuss it just yet. I did ask him if he would be prepared to do a bit of van driving for The Allotmenteers if I asked him. He readily agreed. His heart was as big as the rest of him.

As with Albert Collins, the idea I was fermenting was not strictly legal. I was prepared to cross the line, if it got a result and there was no other option. But I was reluctant to include my allotment mates unless absolutely necessary.

However, I was prepared to include my other mates from my journalist days. They would readily cross the line for me and vice versa. Like me, they would feel that the ends justified the need. Or so I hoped.

Just as I was leaving my curiosity got the better of me. "Have you got any brothers or sisters?" I asked. "You never talk about your family." I was trying to imagine more like Big Mick.

"That's because I don't get on with them. I have a sister and a brother. I see my sister around town but don't see my brother much." He told me.

"Why? Does he live somewhere else?"

"When he was about thirty, he decided he wanted to get healthy. He thought he was getting fat." He looked at me, shaking his head in puzzlement.

"He was only nineteen stones but he wanted to lose a few pounds. He made up his mind that he was going to run five miles a day. That was about eight years ago." He informed me with a smile.

"So why don't you see him?" I thought I was being set up but asked anyway.

"I just told you. He runs five miles a day. He could be anywhere by now." He beamed at me. Hook, line and sinker.

Chapter Fourteen.

Paul Tiler's plot was in good shape. It was well laid out and relatively weed free. He had a problem with Marestail but then so did everyone else on the allotments.

His shed was also in better shape than that of his neighbour Big Mick. His shed had also been burnt down at the same time but he had replaced it with a decent second hand one.

His mouth twitched as he heard the punchline of Big Mick's joke. Subtle jokes like that were what amused him the most. Not that he was often amused.

A loner by nature and preference he liked being on his own.

Over the last year or so however, he had come to appreciate being part of a group.

Apart from Big Mick – strange how nobody called him Mick but always Big Mick – the rest of the guys were in his age bracket. Some friends to chat with now and then was all right.

He came down to the allotment mainly to grow vegetables for himself, wife and family. Any surplus he sold.

During the summer months when salad stuff was required he made a fair bit of money. People always wanted really fresh vegetables and his were always picked daily to order.

Now, as he watched Dave come over, he knew what was going to be discussed. That was the thing he liked about The Allotmenteers. It was a joint effort with everything discussed by everyone before any action was taken.

"Take a pew." He said as Dave Willams came up the path between the two allotments. He indicated the sturdy but worn canvas and aluminium chair, a mate to the one he was sitting on. "Tea?" he asked reaching for his flask.

"No thanks, Paul. I've just had one with Adrian. He tells me he's off to Kent for a few days. Anything to do with Anya Sadlek, you reckon?"

Paul poured himself a cup from the flask. "Well, I do know that her car is in his garage. I saw him driving it in last night. Whether anything is going on or not, I don't know." He paused then continued. "If there is, then I say good luck to him. If there isn't, then there should be. They are a good match, those two."

" I agree. Both have had it hard with their partners and then Kinga. I hope they can find a bit of happiness with each other."

"But, that's not why you are here, is it?" Paul looked up at the guy they all considered their 'gang' leader. "I heard what you and Big Mick were talking about. Why should we get involved?"

"Well, first, because Jan is an allotment holder as well as a shopkeeper. Secondly, we all use the Downeybed shops. Those kids are a nuisance.

 The customers, and most of them are from the Old Folks home opposite, shouldn't have to put up with it. And, if the shops do close, then we will all miss them." Dave argued. Then with a big grin "But, more importantly, it will be fun."

"Ok, I'm in. It'll give us an interest, I suppose. Any ideas?"

"I'm brewing a few ideas but nothing concrete. I'll let you know when I do. Can you have a think about it as well? I asked Big Mick to have a think but he just wants to get physical. Is Pete coming down this morning, do you know?"

"No, he usually only comes down later. Why don't you call in?"

"I've got a bit of tidying to do first. I'll see how the time goes. That Marestail is a bloody nuisance, isn't it?"

Paul drained his cup. "Tell me about it."

Pete Wills was tinkering in his garage cum workshop. He was one of those individuals who, from an early age, pulled things apart to see how they worked or to repair them.

On the work bench in front of him was a brass carriage clock. He had spotted it in a skip as he was walking his dog. He had walked up the path and knocked on the door. The owner had cheerfully agreed that he could have it. "It doesn't work so why keep it?" was the explanation.

He finished tightening the screws on the base and set it down on the bench. He opened a fresh pack of AA batteries and inserted one into the back of the new plastic quartz movement. He nodded in satisfaction as the second hand began to move. The things people threw away.

He would have preferred a brass clockwork movement inside but the plastic quartz substitute worked just as accurately.

And, unless you opened the back, no one would know. Or probably care. Better still a new quartz movement had only cost £3.30 from Ebay.

Twenty minutes or so of not very demanding work and the handsome clock was living again. With a grunt of satisfaction, he put his tools away.

"Pete?" His wife Mary appeared at the door. "Visitor." She indicated Dave Williams behind her. She smiled warmly at Dave and left.

"I guess there is something you want to discuss?" Pete asked as he pulled out a stool. "Allotment business or The Allotmenteers?"

He listened as his visitor explained. Mary had often complained about the number of kids hanging about the shops in the evenings and school holidays.

"Yeah, I'm up for that. Sounds like it could be fun. You want to break into their homes and kidnap them? Or we could get a load of the old people to hang about their homes and pester them for a change?" He grinned.

"Big Mick would be up for the kidnap bit. I'm sure Paul would agree to the second option. Any other ideas? Legal or otherwise?" Dave asked.

"Depends how hard we go in. I take it we don't want the police involved? And we can't hurt them to much?"

"No, I have the beginnings of an idea that doesn't involve violence. Well, not too much. I thought that if we just dealt with the leader or leaders, we could use gentle persuasion to get the whole lot to leave the shops and old folks alone."

"Do we know who is the leader or leaders?" Pete got up and paced. He always thought best when doing something.

"I reckon we have to find that out first before making any concrete plans. Other than that, what is this idea you're cooking in that devious brain of yours?"

After listening to the other's embryo plan, he began to chortle and then laughed out loud. "Yeah." He opinioned. "Yeah, I guess that'll do it. Big time. Remind me never to get on your bad side. Will you?"

He was still smiling as he watched his guest walking down the path.

Dave Williams walked back home. Time to get busy. It looked like The Allotmenteers were going to be back in action again.

Chapter Fifteen.

"Time you got up, Ethan." Lacey Turner shouted from downstairs. There was no response, yet again, so she shouted louder. "ETHAN! GET UP."

Nothing. Oh well, she had tried. Satisfied that her mothering skills were not at fault, she went into the kitchen and made a coffee. Lighting up her third ciggie of the morning, she inhaled deeply, coughed just as deeply and spat the resultant phlegm into the sink.

Ignoring the cups and plates waiting to be washed, she wandered into the living room and resumed watching Jeremy Kyle.

Idly she wondered if she could get onto the show to discuss the problems of parenthood in general and Ethan in particular. A trip down to London and a night in a hotel, all paid for, would be almost as good as a holiday.

She could discuss the problems of bringing up a teenage boy with no father around. The daily hassle of trying to get him up in time for school. The visits from the Social about his truancy. The problems of the constant complaints from her pious neighbours. All kids swore and played loud music, didn't they? He wasn't a bad boy, just a little boisterous sometimes. He just needed a father figure in his life, that's all.

She was out of milk but decided to go to Aldi rather than face that Polish Pratt and his complaints about Ethan and his friends. The constant shoplifting and intimidation of the wrinkley customers from the Old Folks Home over the road that he said Ethan was responsible for.

The Indian shop wasn't any friendlier either. Trying to make out her Ethan was the ringleader of a 'vicious gang of young thugs.' indeed.

Let those two losers try to bring up kids any better. Coming over here and taking jobs off decent hard working English people. They had a bloody nerve complaining to her and accusing Ethan and his friends of all sorts of mischief.

*****

Ethan Turner, ET to his friends, turned over and tried to get back to sleep. Would his mum never learn? What was the point of going to school when there were no jobs when you left? You didn't need any qualifications to be on Jobseekers, did you?

Knowing he would never get back to sleep now, he got up. He looked around for his clothes as he scratched himself vigorously under his boxers.

His room looked a mess. His clothes, clean
and those definitely not, were all over the
floor and on the top of the old cupboard
beside his bed.

Empty crisp packets and drink cans were
piled in and around the overflowing waste
bin. Maybe his mum should spent more time
cleaning his room than shouting at him? The
lazy cow did nothing else all day except
watch those stupid programmes on the telly.

He checked his image in the mirror behind
the door. Soon have chest hair, he thought.
Looked for, and found, a reasonably clean
tee shirt, favourite Bad Boy hoodie, suitably
scruffy jeans and Addy trainers. He sprayed
deodorant generously, in lieu of washing,
gelled his hair and picked at a couple of
spots. Good to go, hot to trot.

He saw a tall, really good looking guy, with
an embryo moustache, deliberately unkempt
black hair and brown bedroom eyes looking
back at him from the mirror when he looked
again. He practised his tough guy, scowly,
face. Yeah, baby , still got it in loads.

He grabbed his phone and checked his
messages.

He was going to have to get some more
credit for his phone soon. That meant going
into town and doing a bit of shoplifting for
stuff he could easily sell on.

Sodding phone ate money but he needed it.
How else was he going to keep in touch with
his mates? What did people use to do?

He thought about his trip into town. He searched his pockets and found only a few pence. Great, that meant he was going to have to walk unless he could get into his mum's purse without her looking. Trouble was the fat cow had started keeping it with her or hiding it from him. Didn't she trust him or something?

He lit the last of the fags he had snitched yesterday from that old bird's bag when she wasn't looking.

 Stupid old bitch leaving the packet right on top of her other shopping. The Wrinkleys deserved to get robbed. He wondered if he could cadge or pinch a few fags from his mum.

It was difficult to get hold of fags now that the shops had started hiding them out of sight in those stupid cupboards.

He finished admiring himself and crept quietly downstairs. Went into the kitchen, grabbed a few biscuits and looked for her purse. No sign of it but her fags were on the worktop. He helped himself to a few and slipped out of the kitchen door and into the garden. The garden fence had a loose board in it that allowed him quick access to the playing fields beyond.

As he began walking towards town, he wondered how long it would be before the dozy mare even noticed that he wasn't in his room.

No wonder his dad had walked out on her. Idly, he wondered if it would have been any different if his dad had been around. To talk to him and take an interest in his life. Too late for that now. He was fifteen and all grown up. What did he need a dad for?

Chapter Sixteen.

"Linzi? It's Grumps…..Yeah, I'm fine. You
ok?……still chasing boys? What are you
going to do if you catch one eh? No, don't go
into detail……..You doing anything tonight?
…No?...good. I'll pop round about eight-
ish……..Because   I need you to do
something for me. ….Well, you'll find out
tonight, won't you?... No, it doesn't involve
helping me on the allotment. See you later
alligator….You're supposed to say In a While
Crocodile….Well, because you are. Ok, I'll
bring some sweets with me. Worthers all
right? No, I wasn't joking…there is nothing
wrong with a Worthers. …you used to love
them when you were younger…..You're how
old now?.....Are you sure? This is Linzi isn't
it?.....Well, if they're old fashioned then I
must be as well……

That's enough of that cheek, young lady.
……Because upsetting an old man who
might, just might, mention you in his will
isn't a very clever move. See you
later……well, wear anything. You don't have
to dress up all the time.

 Something casual that you're not bothered
about getting dirty. No, it doesn't involve
crawling under cars."

Linzi Ellen was my oldest granddaughter
from my older daughter. She was sixteen,
very bright and gorgeous. Which was a worry
for her parents but she was a sensible girl and
knew her own mind. Obviously her looks and
intelligence were passed down from me.

Three years ago she went from being an adorable little girl to a hormonal horror with temper tantrums, door slammings, black walls and a general hostility to anyone whose path crossed hers.

But, we came together as a family. We kept the wrist and leg restraints handy. We contacted the priest. We performed exorcisms. We endured, we held hands and prayed until she came out on the other side and was Nice again.

Now she is, as I often tell her, the joint favourite of my three granddaughters. She refers to herself as The Favourite but, as I told her, "I don't have favourites. I hate you all equally." For some reason, she didn't believe me.

But, given that the other two were six and one, she was definitely my favourite Oldest granddaughter.

I had told her mum that I wanted to borrow her for a while. I didn't tell her why as she doesn't approve of my being down the allotment with my gang of wrinkleys. She feels that I get up to enough mischief on my own without having help.

I had a quick cuppa and then Linzi and I got into my 'party bus' as it is called. This was because I had fitted strips of coloured led lights around the roof interior and wired them into a gizmo that pulsed them in time with the music from the cd player. It has been the Party Bus ever since.

Obviously this customising was done in the winter when I had far too much time on my hands.

As part of the 'I need your help' deal with Linzi, I had to drive through the town centre. She liked the attention.

The bus is very striking with a snazzy paintjob and lots of brightwork. It drew a lot of looks as we drove through town.

Whether from its appearance or because of the coloured interior lights pulsing in time to Black Lace's Agadoo playing through open windows.

Linzi was a bit embarrassed at the choice of music but I had shouted 'bagsy' first so it was my first pick.

My argument is that, if the youngsters can treat we oldies to their, open window, booming crap music,- I'm told the noise is called rap but remain unconvinced - then we oldies are entitled to reciprocate. Or is the word retaliate?

Her embarrassment got worse when we had to stop at the busy pedestrian crossing in North Street.

A bunch of older ladies – I think they are collectively called a 'gossip'- decided halfway across to line up facing us and do the moves.

They were doing well until the end one got a bit too vigorous with her walker, lost her balance and, like ninepins, the whole line collapsed. "Just go Grumps. Now!"

I used to play Gary Glitter's My Gang but have been told that it is now inappropriate. And I don't think anyone, regardless of age, race or colour, should be subjected to Cliff Richard at any time.

My destination was the resident and visitor car park of the Old Folks home opposite the Downeybed shops.

I have that reflective mirror film fitted to the rear windows. You can look out but no one can see in. It is funny looking out and seeing people checking their appearance as they go past without knowing someone is inside watching their every move.

As soon as we arrived we hopped into the middle row seats. These swivel round and are very comfortable.

I didn't know how long we would have to wait before the gang of kids arrived.

Not long as it happened. In my mind I had started to think of them as a Bollock of kids for some reason.

I asked Linzi if she knew any of them from school. She immediately pointed out a hard faced youth of fifteen or sixteen. As you get older it gets harder and harder to tell the age of modern youth.

"That's ET." She said. "Ethan Turner. He's not very nice. When he does attend school, which is not that often, he likes to bully people and cause trouble in class. He's not very popular with the teachers either."

She pointed out and named several others that she recognised but was sure that The Alien was the leader. "It's ET, Grumps" she corrected me.

She also said that he lived just down the road. "You can't miss the house. It's got a front garden full of rubbish. Old tv's, beds, and stuff." She elaborated.

"His mum doesn't do much other than watch tv all day and there is only the two of them living there."

"Ok," I said as I got back into the driving seat. "That's all I wanted to know."

"You could have just taken a few pictures, sent them to my phone and I could have texted you back. That would have been much easier."

I didn't tell her that I had no idea how to text or even if my phone could do that. More likely it would send smoke signals. And how do you get pictures from a camera into a phone? Does the phone develop and print them as well?

I drove her home, gave her the promised Worthers Originals, patted her on the head and asked her to keep everything to herself.

"What are you up to, Grumps?" she asked as exited the bus. "No, on second thoughts, don't tell me. I don't want to know."

As I said, brains and beauty. Definitely my genes. Gotta be.

Chapter Seventeen.

I woke up the next morning which was a good thing.

But, if the idea of going to bed was to sleep then it was a wasted exercise. It was one of those nights when my brain just wouldn't shut off. I dozed on and off then finally got some resemblance of proper sleep for about two hours.

I find this happens a lot when you get old. Gone were the days of sleeping like the dead and waking up suitably refreshed the next morning. But, on the plus side, you do tend to get a lot of thinking done.

Most of my thinking was about the allotment and what to plant – I know, it's sad isn't it? – and, running parallel to this, was working out how best to deal with the Downeybed shop youths.

Many would ask - Lynne would be the first - why should I bother with a problem that wasn't affecting me directly?

I guess it was partly due to the Jesuit Sense of Fair Play that was constantly drummed into me at school. The other part was because it was an interesting exercise. Old age over youth. Brain versus brawn. The sort of challenge that kept the old grey matter ticking over nicely.

The easy part would be to set Big Mick on them and then warn whatever remained to move on and not come back. The hard part was to achieve the same objective without the carnage. But an idea, of sorts, was stirring and evolving. I just had to let it develop by itself.

I often refer to my brain as a computer.

It spends a lifetime amassing information and data then becomes full. In an attempt to make more room, it is constantly deleting stuff or moving around information deemed non-important.

Like where did I put the car keys? Why am I standing on the landing? What day is it and all the similar details that make me look stupid when I can't quickly access them.

The speedy retrieval of information becomes more hit and miss as the previously well ordered logic breaks down due to a lack of storage space.

So, you end up 'forgetting' things due to an inability to quickly retrieve the data you required. You stop mid-sentence because your brain has 'frozen' on a blank page. Just like a computer.

And, just like a computer, shouting at it doesn't help either.

Maybe Lynne just thinks of me as a slow computer sometimes. That would explain the shouting.

Or, maybe your brain is just packing up. Death is, after all, Nature's way of telling you to slow down.

Whatever analogy you think suits best, the one thing I have found to help is to think of something else. Leave the old computer or grey matter to sort itself out in its own good time.

So, I was planning what to plant this warm early March morning as I enjoyed my tea sitting outside my allotment shed.

Even though the weather was warm, there was always the chance of a late frost.

To be on the safe side, I decided to pot plant broad beans, tomatoes, lettuce and similar fragile stuff.

 Plant the seeds and grow them in a container in the greenhouse I added last year. Plant later when the weather was more summery. Simples.

Shallots and garlic I could plant out straight away. I used a lot of garlic in both cooking and in garlands hanging around the door to my room. I did think of adding a cross but the garlic seems to be working ok for now.

I could put some covers over the raised beds to warm them up for my early plants and seeds. Get some carrots, cabbages, cauliflowers and other reasonably hardy stuff planted towards the end of the month. Busy, busy, busy.

But, at the moment, the sun was out, my tea was just right, the birds were singing and the clouds were floating lazily across the sky. What more could an addled old man want? I wondered.

A bit more peace and quiet was my first thought as I heard my name being called from further down the path. Now what was up? I looked down towards the main gate and saw Lynne waving.

I had the keys so she couldn't get into the allotment because the gates are always locked after use to stop non plot holders getting in. But, given the holes in the perimeter fence, that was probably a waste of time.

I didn't hurry down. I sauntered, thereby giving the impression that I was in charge and would come when I wanted, not when I was called. I waved to Pete as I passed. This time, I was wrong, very wrong.

She was clearly in a state. She beckoned towards the car as I eventually reached her. "It's Penny." She said. "She is in a bad way. We need to get her to the vet. I thought you would want to come."

She was right. We have five Yorkshire terriers. No, we are not collectors but used to be breeders. Unlike a lot of dog breeders, once a bitch is past producing a litter, we keep them and don't just discard them. They live out the rest of their lives with us in a comfortable retirement.

Yorkies tend to be long lived and Penny was no exception. She was sixteen and in robust good health. Or so we thought. But, looking at her in a travel cage in the back of the car, this was obviously not the case.

She was panting and dribbling copiously. Worse, she seemed very disorientated.

"What happened?" I asked as I got in the driver's seat. I had shouted up for Pete to lock up the plot for me.

"She was fine but then her back legs seemed to give way and she couldn't walk properly. When she did move, it was round in circles. She was a bit lethargic earlier on but that is reasonably normal so I didn't take much notice."

It is true. Old Yorkies can sleep for England. They don't seem to need much exercise although they are always eager for a walk if you want to take them.

Penny was sixteen and, given the usually held belief that one dog year is equal to seven human, was also 112 years old in that ratio. Perfectly normal to sleep a lot. But, when not sleeping, she was as sharp as a kitchen knife. Always ready to eat, play or just carry out her duties as the pack leader. So the disorientation was a worry.

The vet practice was nearby so we weren't long getting there. They are usually good in seeing emergency cases and the other waiting owners never seem to mind a really sick animal queue jumping.

Once on the examination table, we got asked a lot of questions whilst the vet gave her the once over.

Yes, she was eating fine. No, there were no bowel or bladder problems. Yes, she took an interest in her surroundings.

Yes, it came on suddenly. No, she hadn't, as far as we were aware, eaten anything toxic. Yes, the other animals were fine.

He spent a long time listening to her heart and lungs with his stethoscope. When he looked up, I already knew the answer.

One of the sadder aspects of keeping pets is situations like this. Over the years, I had taken a lot of dogs to the vets and, as they got older, the diagnoses were inevitable.

So, I knew what was coming. I think Lynne did as well. I usually tried to shield her from vet experiences like this and went alone when I already suspected what the end result would be.

"It's her heart. It's very fluttery and weak." was the verdict. "That's why she seems out of it and can't walk very well. Because her heart isn't pumping properly, her brain and blood aren't getting enough oxygen. Less oxygen to the brain means it can't function properly. The same way the muscles can't function without oxygenated blood."

We discussed treatments. There weren't many options. There were drugs that would ease things temporarily but, apart from the cost, the outcome would only be delayed.

And, no, the cost of the treatment wasn't a deciding factor. If there was even a chance of a successful treatment, we would sell all we had to pay for it. But, there was no wonder drug. No way of getting past the basic problem. Penny had just got old.

What we could do for her was simple. Simple but heartbreaking. Penny was in distress and there was no other option.

I signed the consent form. Stroked her as the vet shaved her foreleg. She looked at me and, for a moment, the old Penny was there and looking at me with her knowing eyes. She had briefly returned to me.

She licked my hand as if to say 'thanks for a great life. I've loved it and you. I know it is hard but thank you for doing this for me.' It was almost as if she knew what was coming. Knew, accepted it and forgave us.

The vet nodded and I picked her up. Lynne was crying. She gave Penny a final pat. I had done this before but it never got any easier. The vet placed a tourniquet around her shaven leg.

I held her against my chest as the needle went into the vein and the plunger was slowly depressed.

I stroked her and felt her relax as the anaesthetic entered her bloodstream. I watched with tears streaming down my cheeks as her eyes closed for the very last time. I actually felt, as I had done many times before, the exact moment she left us. She just went limp and, somehow, empty.

One moment she was here, the next she wasn't. Her soul, her presence, her essence went from her. There was no pain, no stress. Penny had simply crossed over that divide from our hearts and life and into our memories. One of the few times that I hoped there was some kind of afterlife where we would meet again.

Lynne and I had done our last kind act to yet another valued member of our family.

People may say that she was just a dog. Those people obviously weren't, couldn't be, dog owners.

How can an animal live with you for sixteen years and not become part of you? As we put Penny into the car, my mind flooded with my memories of her.

Sixteen years ago another of our bitches, Milly, gave birth to two pups. Yorkies generally don't tend to have large litters and also have a high mortality rate. Out of a larger litter, we always tended to lose the weakest runt. No matter what we did, feeding hourly by bottle included, it became a losing battle.

Milly had her two pups and lost one within the morning. Sometimes they just are just too weak and give up. The remaining pup seemed to flourish although it was a bit smaller than normal. But, two days later, that one had died as well.

Milly was distraught. She refused to eat and just lay there with her litter blanket. She obviously got something from the smell her two pups had left on it but it wasn't enough to comfort her.

She began to lose weight and be obsessed with the blanket. She wouldn't let us take it away and actually got quite aggressive if we tried to do so.

This behaviour was so far removed from her normally placid and friendly behaviour as to be worrying.

I began to look on the internet for Yorkie puppies and, after a long search, eventually located a dealer in Leeds who had two five week old pups.

I put Milly in a travel cage and set off. The weather was atrocious with ice and fog on the motorway.

It was in that empty period just between Christmas and the New Year so, thankfully, traffic was light. I arrived at the breeder's house and went to see the two pups.

I had already told her what the problem was and that I wanted to take one back with me if Milly accepted it. Normally pups don't leave their mums until eight weeks but Milly still had milk. So, provided she accepted the pup, she could feed it.

I looked at the two little bitch pups and had another dilemma.

Which one? I had thought of buying both but one of them was already promised. Which one I choose didn't matter.

My selection method was simple but, I had found, effective. Both pups looked the same. Both adorable little scraps of black and tan. I clicked my fingers and one looked up and tried to waddle over to investigate. That little bitch was Penny.

We introduced the pup to Milly cautiously. Milly might have tried to kill it if she saw it as a threat. Instead it went the way I hoped. She accepted the pup joyously and, after having sniffed it, lay down to feed it. The pup accepted her as a source of food and Milly was content.

I paid the £300 breeder discounted price and set off on the much less anxious journey home. Penny was so called because the first thing she did when Lynne picked her up was to pee, or spend a penny, on her.

At three months old, Penny broke her right foreleg and, after extensive and expensive surgery, came home a week later with a blue cast on her leg. Fortunately the pet insurance paid the £2000 plus vet bill.

Within minutes of being home, she was jumping on and off the furniture. Her cast no impediment to her joy at being reunited with us again.

It quickly became clear that Penny was an exceptional little dog. She had the thickest and nicest coat. She was bright, sociable and had an infectious sense of fun. People who say dogs don't have sense of humour obviously haven't had a Yorkie as a pet.

She quickly choose me as her favourite and followed me everywhere. When I went for my yearly bath, I would finally open the door and there she was, waiting.

If I went down the garden to my workshop she would be there a few minutes later. Peering round the door, checking to see that I was all right.

When I went away for a day or two on a job or press trip, she would mope around until I returned.

Lynne always knew when I was returning because Penny would get excited and wait by the door for as much as 20 minutes before I got home. There was an almost telepathic bond between us.

When she had her first litter of three, she would bring each pup in her mouth to me. Deposit each one carefully in my lap and look at me as if to say 'Keep an eye on them for me.' Content that they would be safe, she went about her business in the garden or got something to eat.

She was my shadow, my wingman and my friend for sixteen long companionable years. Her 'mum' Milly passed away in her sleep two years ago and Penny would still go up the garden and sit on her grave.

Now, I was bringing her home for the last time. She would join her mum. I dug an grave for her next to Milly. Penny would like it there. It was sheltered and got the morning sun. There are eleven dog graves in our garden. Each one marked with a cross, a little plaque and a flagstone.

Each year on the anniversary of their deaths, we put a flower on their graves. Stupid, sentimental? Not to us. They were part of our family and we still remembered and missed them. Now there would be twelve graves.

I dug Penny's grave and laid her in it. I had wrapped one of my old tee shirts around her. I slowly and carefully filled it in and laid a paving slab over it.

I got my drill and fixed the wooden cross to the wall behind it. When I was next in town, I would get a metal plaque with her name and dates engraved on it and put that on the cross. My last duty and pleasure to my old friend who would be greatly missed and fondly remembered.

Inside we were both subdued. The remaining four dogs quickly picked up on our mood. They searched the house for Penny, their leader. They came to us and licked our hands. They seemed to understand what had happened and mourned with us.

Zak is Penny's son from her very last litter. He had the same wonderful thick coat and the same qualities.

Now Penny would live on in him. I looked at him lying in my lap and almost automatically looked around for his mum.

Normally she would be at my feet. It was odd not seeing her there. I could see a lot of Penny in Zak and that would be bring back both the good and the sad memories.

The fact that most of our pups were sold locally meant that we were always meeting people who had offspring from our dogs.

Penny's pups were always distinctive and easily recognisable. Her last bitch pup, Zak's sister, went to live with an elderly couple in nearby Daventry.

Six months later they brought her back to visit us. Bluebell turned out to be exactly the same as a younger Penny.

If nothing else, Penny would live on in her pups. As for us, we had decided that there would be no more new dogs. Lynne and I were both getting on and didn't want to leave any pets behind when we went.

When the time was right, I would get out the vhs tapes I had made of Penny when she first came to us. And all the subsequent little snippets of recordings through the years since then. At the right time, I could enjoy watching them with a smile on my face and a tear in my eyes. But not now. It was too soon. Now they would just depress and upset me.

Feeding time was another reminder. I automatically got out and filled five bowls with dog food. Counted them, belatedly remembered and fought the great wave of sadness that threatened to overwhelm me.

Later that evening, after a very quiet evening meal, I got in Lynne's car to run up to the shops for some milk. My bus was in the garage and I couldn't be bothered to get it out. Normally I would walk but I just wasn't in the mood today.

Outside Jan's shop was the usual crowd of rowdy youngsters. They had some loud music going and there was a lot of noise. Some were dancing, if their strange movements could be called dancing. I couldn't see anything to play music on so maybe they were hearing music in their heads. No doubt strange voices as well. But then I noticed that the dancers had string coming from their ears into a little square box. I guessed it was a little radio or maybe a tape recorder.

I dimly remember my granddaughter showing me a similar box and calling it a Highpad or something like that. She also said that the little box could hold thousands of recordings. I knew she was joking so didn't bite. Thousands of records indeed. She must think I was getting senile.

The rest of the mob were smoking and drinking from cans.

They tried to get me to buy them more drinks and fags. They got angry when I just ignored them. They crowded around me, jeering and jostling.

I wasn't in the mood for them and just pushed my way angrily through them. A couple stumbled and fell. I ignored their noisy complaints and carried on.

Inside I got my milk from Jan but didn't stop to chat. He saw I wasn't in a talkative mood and walked with me to the door.

I guessed he was going to have a smoke as his lighter was in his hands. Outside the gang of youths were noisily running down the road. One stopped and called out to us "That'll teach you Grandad.". It was ET.

I said goodbye to Jan and walked to the car. Both driver's side tyres were flat. I turned to the other side. They were flat as well. And, not just flat but slashed across their walls. Bastards.

I used Jan's phone to call Lynne first then my mate Eamon. He has a scrap business and has a car transporter to collect scrap cars. He was the guy who supplied the van that I used to accumulate all those speeding tickets on Collins' behalf last year.

He came as quickly as he could and loaded Lynne's car on to his vehicle and dropped it of at my house.

Tomorrow morning I would jack up the car, put it on axle stands and get the wheels off and the tyres changed. Great.

I had only replaced them all a couple of months ago and would now have to spend another £280 on replacements.

An expensive day. Nearly £400 with the vet's bill.

I thought about calling the police but what was the use? There was no way of knowing which of the mob had actually slashed the four tyres.

Lynne was fuming when I told her it would be a waste of time. She was all for going after the mob and sorting them out. I did think of letting her. Instead, I calmed her down and we went back inside.

There was no doubt now in my mind that they would get sorted. What was someone else's problem had now become mine.

Now it was personal and now they would pay. ET in particular.

But, for now, all I wanted to do was remember my little wingman and mourn for her. Tomorrow was another day and revenge is a dish best served cold.

Chapter Eighteen.

After yet another sleepless night, I got up around 5.30. I had spent the night grieving and remembering the good times with Penny. It would take time.

Normally when I go down stairs in the morning, the dogs are waiting to greet me. This morning, they just stayed in their beds. I automatically counted them. Zak, Cassie, Milly and Monty. I went to look round for Penny and then stopped.

Penny had a thing for feet. From being a little pup, she loved licking feet. Every morning she would lick my feet, her thick tail waving her body as she excitedly greeted me. Now I guess I would have to wash my own feet.

Even as the thought crossed my mind, I recognised it as a good sign.

I was beginning to accept my loss and remember the good times. Time to move on. Idly I wondered, as I guess most older people do, whether anyone would miss me.

And, again as with most people, I wondered how my demise would come about. Nice and peacefully I hoped. Maybe I would go in my sleep, like my grandfather. Here one minute, gone the next. Close your eyes, quick and painless. Don't feel a thing.

Although I guess it wasn't quite the same for the passenger in his car at the time.

Anyway, I went down the allotment for around 6.30. I love these quiet mornings. Nature at its best. A cup of tea, birds singing, the early mist going as the weak sun became stronger.

I pottered in the green house. I had bought it off a departing guy who had given up on the Good Life.

I had to move it from the bottom plots to the exalted top plots. Initially I had thought of dismantling it but Big Mick had another solution.

A shovel under one corner, lift and place a brick under the structure. He did the same with the other corners. Ready.

With the greenhouse raised, we slid a couple of scaffolding poles down it's length. Big Mick is strong but my strength is his equal.

It's just one of those things. I might look old and weak but I have an inbuilt natural strength that has fooled a lot of people.

We stepped inside the poles at either end, grabbed, lifted and sedan chaired it to its new home. Simple but effective. A bit like the pair of us.

Now I was potting seeds. Getting them started ready for planting next month.

Even with the weak spring sunlight, the green house was warming up nicely. Old White Hair Adrian shared the greenhouse with me as there was plenty of room. I wondered how he was getting on down in Kent.

I know he had rung Pete, who lived almost opposite, told him where the spare key was and asked if he could go in and feed his aquarium fish. He hadn't mentioned the where, the who or the how longs.

I finished in the greenhouse and put the kettle on for another cuppa.

Several people turned up and wandered around. Some to work, some to pretend to work and some to wonder whether the allotment and/or they would work. There was a lot of other people's plots being inspected. Several people were discussing planting tactics and the group buying of seeds.

A lot of them hadn't visited during the winter months and, like hibernators waking after a long sleep, were walking round distractedly and analyzing the damage caused by frost, neglect and the occasional vandal. Most of us had go off relatively lightly due to the mild winter.

I saw Big Mick scurrying to his hide with a Greggs logo'ed bag firmly grasped. I guessed he had just come off the night shift and was getting his allotment breakfast before going home to get his official one.

Paul, as always, was beavering away. His plot was always in tip top condition as he relied on it for his supplementary income.

Jan Hawk'nspit entered the main gate, saw me sitting down, enjoying the strengthening sun, and walked up.

He asked how I was after the tyre slashing incident. I made him a coffee and told him why I was a bit off last night.

I guess that Poles don't have the same affection for pets as we do. He suggested I could just get another dog. I could see he was itching to broach another subject so gave him his head.

"Have you spoken to your friends about those bollocking kids?" he finally asked.

The conversations I have with Jan are usually a mix of English, German, Polish and sign language. For brevity, I translate as best I can.

I told him I had and asked him how often he got a delivery from Poland and how it worked. Was it a single drop or did the driver have several deliveries around the UK? He thought about it.

"Sometimes just a single delivery up here after delivering the bulk of the load to a London wholesaler. Sometimes it is just part of a groupage load."

He knew I was an ex driver so didn't explain what groupage was. To those of you unlucky enough not to be truckers, let me explain.

It means that a company collects lots of little consignments going to a particular area or country. These are called groupage.

When there have enough for a full load, a truck picks them all up and the driver either delivers them himself or drops the whole load off at a similar groupage specialist in the destination area or country.

It is a cost effective and well tried method of delivering goods not large enough to warrant their own truck.

"Does the driver ring you before hand to arrange delivery or just turn up?" I asked.

" I receive an email or phone call the day before delivery."

"And, are the drivers usually Polish?"

"Yes, most of my deliveries are from a Polish company called Groupa Oscar. You have heard of them , yes?"

Indeed I had. A Polish company that had mushroomed after the Berlin Wall came down and the West's Free Trade system replaced communism.

Like of a lot of the eastern Bloc transport companies, they were able to substantially increase their profits and still undercut the Western competition.

"Do you know any of the drivers well enough to get them to do something illegal for you?" I asked.

Jan laughed. "Foo Kinell, truck drivers haven't changed since our driving days. Offer them enough money and they will do anything. Well, most things." He looked across at me. "Why do you ask?"

"I can't tell you just yet but, when are you expecting your next delivery?"

"Next week. Usually around Wednesday or Thursday."

"Ok, I'll talk to you Saturday or Sunday. I have to speak to my friends and see if anything can be arranged."

He look suddenly worried. "You're not going to get anyone killed, are you?"

I didn't answer him. Nothing like a bit of suspense. I just told him I had to go into town to get some new tyres sorted.

He offered to chip in but I told him it was ok. Truck drivers, eh? Salt of the earth.

The rest of the day seemed to be taken up with getting the tyres changed. This involved jacking the car up with my trolley jack, removing two wheels and taking them into town for new tyres. Return, refit and do the same for the two remaining wheels.

I also popped into a shop in town to get a plaque made up for Penny.

It was one of those 'while you wait' shops but I gave the guy the instructions on my first tyre run and picked up the finished item on the second.

I decided to get a bit more than the usual name and date plaque I usually got. I know you shouldn't have favourites but Penny had always been mine.

It was like when you tend to favour one of your children over the others. You know you shouldn't but it just happens.

From the moment the young Penny came to investigate my snapping fingers, the bond between us was created.

After finishing with the car and putting my stuff away, Lynne and I finished Penny's grave. We laid bricks around the perimeter and put some white gravel between the bricks and the flagstone.

We do this for all the dogs that have lived and died in the 31 years we have been in this house. I've told Lynne I'll do the same for her when the time comes. She gave me one of her Looks.

Finally I put up the plaque. It simply read:

Penny, sleep well my little mate,

You've earned your rest.

Our time together was short but great.

I'll always miss you. You were the best.

A great wave of sadness threatened to overcome me as I put away the tools. It was stupid but it was an ingrained habit that made me look around for her as I walked into the house. I knew it would take time. A lot of time.

Chapter Nineteen.

ET still remembered the look on the old wrinkley's face. The feeling as the knife went home and the hiss of escaping air. That would teach the oldies to show him a little respect. Teach them not to mess with ET and his crew.

He was at home getting something to eat. There wasn't much in the kitchen. There never was this late into the week.

The old cow spent most of her giro on fags and booze. He got a couple of slices of stale bread and made some toast. In the fridge was a half tin of beans. He found a reasonably clean plate. He poured the beans over the toast and put the plate in the stained microwave.

A few minutes later he was finished. Leaving the dirty plate on the table, he went out of the kitchen and through the gap in the fence into the playing fields beyond. Already he could see his crew hanging around the skateboard area.

As usual no one had any money, fags or food. Time for another trip up to the shops.

There were usually around fifteen in his crew. Sometimes more, sometimes less. The more there were, the more successful they became. Either as a concerted grab and run on one of the shops or by harassing and distracting a wrinkly whilst grabbing their groceries or cash.

The two running the shops, the Pole and the Indian, had given up calling the cops. There was no point. As soon as the pigmobile appeared, they would split up and run off in all directions.

Now the two foreigners did their best to keep them out by manning the doors and refusing entry. But they had to serve customers and there was always a chance to grab something then.

Sometimes, they would hang around the chippie and snatch someone's food as they struggled with the door. But that was getting harder and harder as the customers wised up.

As a last resort, they could always go into town and mug someone once it got a bit darker. Usually someone old who wouldn't resist or someone younger who would be too scared to try.

In the meantime, Brittany would provide a welcome diversion. Either her or Tahita. Both of them were always up for it. One day he'd have them both together. He put on a swagger as he walked up to his crew.

Chapter Twenty.

The next morning Adrian appeared at my shed door as normal. I wasn't expecting him. I added another cup and tea bag.

"I thought you were down in Kent for a few days?" I asked.

He took the cup and sat down heavily. He seemed unsettled like he had a lot on his mind. "I was".

I waited but there was nothing else forthcoming. "So, it didn't go well between you and Anya?" I prompted.

"How did you know about that?"

"Not just me. Pete and Paul have guessed as well. Paul saw her car in your garage and Pete 1471'd your phone call to him. It was a Kent area code." Why, does it matter if you are seeing Anya? She's a nice lady."

He drank some tea, started to say something then drank some more. Finally he looked at me and then away again. "Yes, she is. She's a very nice lady."

"And that worries you because…?"

He drained his cup and put it down. "This is private, right? Just between us. No broadcasting it around the allotment. Not even to the others." His eyes searched mine looking for confirmation.

"Yeah, sure. If that's what you want." I agreed.

Yes, she is a nice lady." He continued. "We have been spending a bit of time together when she comes up to see the Memorial. We got chatting casually at first. About the weather and how nice Kinga's garden is looking and how much she appreciated it

. Gradually I looked forward to seeing her again. I used to watch out for her from my kitchen window." He turned to look at his house as if I needed to know where it was. "I would invite her in for a cup of tea and to freshen up." He explained.

"About two months ago, I suggested we went out for something to eat before she drove home."

He got up and started pacing. " It was nice. We got along great. She's funny, educated, pretty and she makes me laugh. And that's the problem".

"Sorry, mate, but I can't see any problem. You get on well together. She's free, you're free. You're both well over 21. Why is there a problem?"

He looked at me and his face was sad again. When he had been talking about Anya, it had been happy.

Suddenly, my tired old brain hiccupped up an idea and everything became clear. I remembered what he had told me a few days ago.

" Adrian, sit down mate and look at me." I must have spoken a bit sharply because he just dropped into the seat again.

" I guess I know what the problem is. You feel guilty, don't you? You feel that you are being disrespectful to Gwen, don't you?" I looked over. He didn't meet my eyes but just nodded. I could see he was getting emotional again.

"Look, I am going to say something now. I want you to listen and I don't want you to interrupt. Ok?" He nodded again.

"You told me the other day that is was you and Gwen's wedding anniversary. Also, the sixth anniversary of her death." He flinched at the last word.

"You were both happy together right? And you've been faithful to her memory ever since?" Again a little nod.

"But, what if the situation was reversed? What if it was you who had cancer and knew you only had a short time left? What would you do for Gwen?" He was really listening now.

"It goes without saying that you would see her comfortably off. Get your affairs in order, get all the planning done. Take as much stress and responsibility off her as you could, right?"

"Yes" he said softly. "Yes, I would."

"Course you would. We all would. And, I guess you would do something else as well. A couple as close as you two. You'd worry about her, wouldn't you? You know, afterwards. Worry that she'd be ok." I stole a quick glance at him. He was listening.

" You'd ask one of us to keep an eye out for her. You would want her to get on with her life. Get a little happiness and not waste her final years mourning you. You'd want her to find someone nice to look after her, protect her and just be there for her to talk to when she needed to, wouldn't you?" I saw that he could see where I was heading.

" I bet that Gwen had a very similar conversation with you, right?"

He looked over. Already his eyes were moist. He just nodded.

"Right, you cared for her. She cared for you and how you'd cope afterwards as well. I bet she told you to find someone else and not just mourn her for the rest of your life, right? Just as you would have told her the same thing."

He was crying softly now. "Yeah" he managed in a thick voice. "Yeah, we had that conversation. I told her I would but I didn't mean it. I thought it would comfort her. She was so brave. All that suffering and she was still thinking of me. I didn't want anyone else. I wanted her."

"I know mate, I know. But, something changed when Anya came on the scene,. didn't it? You started to get feelings for another woman." Again a little nod.

"And now you feel as if you have been unfaithful to Gwen. To her memory." His hands clenched and unclenched the chair arms as he struggled to hold it together.

" Well, I don't think so, Adrian. I think you have mourned long enough. No one could accuse you of forgetting about Gwen.

But, you can still remember her and be happy as well. She would have wanted that. You just told me she wanted you to find someone and get on with your life."

I took a swig of nearly cold tea. My throat was getting dry with all this talking. Adrian was quiet now. Listening.

"And, there's not just you now." I continued. He looked at me questioningly.

"There is also Anya. She lost both her husband and her daughter. I bet she had the same conversation with her husband towards the end as well. And I bet she is feeling the same guilt as you, right?"

"Yes, she told me it didn't feel right. But we get on so well. We laugh at the same things. Like the same stuff. I love her funny little accent.

She says she likes my white hair. We have so much in common and yet,   it's like there is this wedge between us."

"Yeah and there always bloody will be if you two don't come to your senses." I said sharply. He sat up.

"You have a choice. Get together or both of you be unhappy. Both of you can be miserable or happy.

. What do you think Gwen would prefer?
Anya's husband? Kinga? I can tell you now,
with absolutely no hesitation, they would
want you both to be happy." I told him.

" What are the chances of someone from
Kent meeting a miserable old git from Rugby
if not for fate? Don't waste it, you daft old
bugger. Get on the phone to her now. Better
still, get in your bloody car now and drive
down there. And don't come back until she
has said yes. Now go."

For a moment I thought it was going to get
violent. But he stopped and thought for a
moment. "Can you keep an eye on the all….."

"Yes. Just go. Now!" Suddenly he was
smiling. He patted me on the shoulder and
began walking towards his house.

I called after him. He stopped and turned.
Looked at me. 'Now what?' I could almost
hear him thinking. 'You going to shout at me
a bit more?'

"Take some more advice. Get to a chemist
and get some Grecian 2000. It'll take bloody
years off you. White hair doesn't suit you.
The ladies don't like it really."

He grinned broadly and stuck two fingers up.
I waved him off. Went back to my stone cold
tea and decided to make another one. I had
the time. Didn't have to be anywhere fast.
Not like my old friend.

As I lit the gas ring. I idly wondered if there
was an opposite of Grecian 2000. Something
that would turn your hair white.

I sat and drank. Thought about what I was going to do next. Both on the allotment and to those bollocking kids. The allotment was easy. The kids perhaps not so.

 But, for the moment, the sun was up, my feet were up and my plan was percolating through nicely. Just perfick as Pop Larkin used to say in the Darling Buds of May.

I thought idly of stuff to do on the allotment. Idly being the operative word.

 I didn't feel like doing much more than what I was already doing: just enjoying the day. I closed my eyes. Five or ten minutes wouldn't hurt surely?

I remember sitting down, putting my feet up on the shelf/work area and leaning back. I remember there was a little robin, who came visiting for food, scolding me in the background. Wanting to be fed. Wait you cheeky little bugger, I thought. I'll get you something in a few minutes.

The sun got warmer. I relaxed even more. The outside worlds began to fade slowly away. Softly and silently.

Chapter Twenty One.

"Dave. Dave Williams." Someone was shouting from the front gate. Then there was the sweetest sound ever made. To a truckdriver, that is. The twin blast of a truck's air horns.

The eurgh-eurgh siren call had me awake, up and walking down to the top gate in seconds. Come to me, come to me, it seemed to say.

"I knew that'd wake you up, you old bugger." A deep voice said. "Lynne said you'd be down here sleeping."

I had already recognised the distinctive voice of Clive Pindred. I'd spent weeks on end listening to it as we did one road development test after another.

Clive was in his mid 50's. Tall, well built and, to make matters worse, a Ginger. Ginger hair tied back in a ponytail. Ginger beard obscuring most of his face. Great tufts of the stuff sprouting out of his shirt front.

He grinned as he saw me. It wasn't reassuring. More like a grizzly greeting you with knife and fork in hand. He stuck out his hand and I gripped it warily. Sometimes it took days for the feeling to return after shaking hands with Clive.

Today he was in a good mood. I reckoned I would have full feeling back within the hour. I'm a weedy looking old guy but with a more than average natural strength. Clive is a very large, tough looking guy with almost superhuman natural strength.

"Hello Clive." I said as, trying not to wince, I massaged some feeling back into my right hand. "You got my message then?"

"Sure did, you old bugger." He said in his 'several tones deeper than Barry White' voice. The ladies loved his voice for some reason. I guess if he had white hair he'd be irresistible. "What's up?"

I looked at his sleeper cab ERF truck parked up behind him. It was a left hooker - left hand drive – and didn't really look up to much. There were several deep scratches along the front bumper. The cab was painted in a very faded diarrhoea brown colour.

There were dents on the door and mismatched driving mirrors hanging from their arms. Rust had visibly eaten away at several of the larger body panels.

It looked like it was on its way to the scrap yard and the big question would be whether the scrap man would accept or not.

But, I had driven this vehicle many times myself. Had driven thousands of miles in it and would not hesitate to drive it again.

I took Clive up to my shed and made yet another brew.

The thought crossed my mind about opening a little café on the allotment. Get Lynne down to cook and serve hot food. It would keep her busy and she would meet some nice people.

It was an idea I instantly dismissed. These people were, after all, my friends. It wouldn't be right.

I gave Clive his cup and we sat down. We were old mates and we talked and caught up with what each of us was doing.

*****

I had first met Clive many years ago when we were both international truckers. It was an on-off friendship like those of most long distance drivers. We would see each other in some lay by, industrial estate or other location somewhere in europe.

It might be weeks before we met again or we could spend weeks travelling together on the epic overland treks to Saudi Arabia.

On those trips you had to rely completely on your fellow drivers and there was a bond between us that never disappeared.

When I came off the road I was at a loss. Driving was my life and the one thing I was good at. I had my own truck and trailer and well paid steady work. Due to a simple eye infection I lost the sight in my right eye.

Now, I don't know if you have ever suffered the same loss or even had to keep one eye closed for any period of time. If you have, you will know that the first thing you lose is perspective. Your brain is struggling to interpret images from one eye when it was used to two.

Driving was a nightmare and could be potentially lethal. I tried to continue driving but couldn't. In my mind I would be correctly positioned in the road and driving well. Then I would look into the driving mirror and find I was way out of the white lane markings. Dangerously so.

 I was just wandering from lane to lane as I tried to drive in a straight line. I couldn't do it and gave up. When you know yourself that you are driving dangerously, then it is definitely time to give up.

So I sold my business and found myself at home and trying to think of a way to earn a living. It wasn't easy for someone of my age, just over 45, with no real skills.

 A local company, EconomyKruising, made speed controls for cars and trucks and were advertising for part-time engineers in the local paper. Experience in driving hgv's would be particularly welcome.

It was local so I applied. I got the job and found myself liking it and was good at it. I made several cost cutting suggestions that went down well. The only problem was that the pay wasn't very good compared to what I was used to.

As time went on, I gradually came to terms with my eye loss and my brain adapted. Within six months I was back driving trucks again. Just the unit at first and then with the trailer attached.

Only this time I was demonstrating the firm's truck –which was fitted with the speed control equipment – to various transport companies, fleet engineers and transport magazines.

Again I was good at it because I was a truck driver, could fit the equipment and talk equally to both a driver and a fleet engineer as I demonstrated it.

One day one of those Do I or Don't I chances came along. I was demonstrating to the editor of a truck driver magazine and we got chatting about other things.

Within minutes we found we were kindred spirits. We had both been international drivers, both done the Saudi runs and were both passionate about trucks and trucking.

He suggested that I write an article about starting up as an owner driver. The problems, the rewards, that sort of thing.

My first thought was that I couldn't do it. I read a lot of books but didn't have a clue about writing. He persuaded me to give it a try and said he would edit if for me.

So I pecked out the 2000 words on an old typewriter and posted it off to him. I didn't hear anything so presumed it was rubbish and forgot about it.

Two months later, I opened this magazine and found my article as the lead feature.

And, as I found out as I proudly read through it, with virtually nothing added or taken away from it.

I was so proud I thought I would burst. I rang the guy to thank him and he instantly gave me more work. He told me I was wasting my time where I was and should be writing full time. I said I couldn't afford to take the chance. I needed regular pay.

Then, once again, fate stepped in and I was made redundant. The company closed it's non profitable speed control section to concentrate on its profitable mainstream engineering work.

I was given six months pay in lieu of redundancy. This was a generous sum given that I had only been there seven months. More importantly, it gave me a six month financial buffer to try and make it as a transport journalist.

Bear with me, I will get to Clive in a minute or three. I'm just laying down some background. You'll appreciate it later on.

Well within the six months, I was making good money as a transport journalist.

As both a driver and an owner driver I was an oddity.

I could write for a driver, an owner driver or a fleet engineer with the experience and authority that comes from having done the job.

I got asked to test more and more new trucks as they came out. I would test them for driver comfort, fuel economy, ease of servicing and general overall impressions.

As an owner driver I had to buy my own fuel so I became very good at driving very economically.

As a driver, I had spent many hours and nights in a sleeper cab and knew what worked and what didn't.

As a, operator who did most of his own maintenance work, I appreciated a truck's easy access and maintenance capabilities.

With a combination of all three qualities, I became a good writer, developed my own style, and knew what drivers and engineers were looking for.

Pretty soon I was an accepted, - and dare I say it? Yeah why not, It was true.- and respected journalist by the trade, the manufacturers and the truckers.

Because of my rapidly returning driving abilities, I began to get excellent fuel economy and journey times from the trucks I tested. These tended to be better than those obtained by my fellow truck testers and made me very popular with the truck manufacturers.

Soon they began to approach me to carry out some driving on the new trucks, engines or drivelines they were developing.

Again, because of my background, I could make suggestions about driver comfort – always something I cared passionately about – and other things that could improve the truck, its economy, its safety or anything else I thought needed improving.

Some suggestions went down well. Others were shelved on cost issues. But, I was getting a reputation as a truck tester.

I began to appear in the truck manufacturer promotion videos. I went on tours of transport cafes with the latest trucks to talk about them and answer the trucker's questions in a common language.

Eventually I was approached by an engine manufacturer to undertake a month long development test on its new engine.

Only this time it was just me who was providing everything. The test comparison vehicles, the drivers, the route, the whole kit and kerboodle. It was a hectic three months leading up to the start of the tests.

They gave me a good budget and I hired two trucks and three trailers for the duration. I took the trucks up to Feathers in Halifax to get them set up on a rolling road. This was to ensure that the trucks were operating at manufacturer specifications.

The route I outlined on a map and then drove it in my car to see if it would work. I wanted motorways, dual carriageways, A-roads, quiet country roads and a stop/ start city traffic section. It needed hills, twists and turns and straight stretches.

It came in at just under 250 miles and represented a trucks average daily route and distance.

There were three thirty minute breaks during the day with readings taken at each stop. I was happy with it.

I got the trucks and trailers together at the manufacturer's factory. The manufacturer provided its own truck with the new engine installed. I loaded each truck and trailer to precisely its legal operating weight and weight distribution.

I got independent engineers in to check the trailers, the trucks and to install fuel measuring equipment. I wanted no hint of favouritism or unfair criticism.

If the trucks or trailers needed anything doing it was done. New tyres, new brake linings, whatever was required to get them into to peak condition.

When all that was done I needed two other drivers. I had already spoken to the two I had in mind and one of them was Clive Pindred. The other was John Slater.

I knew both of them and knew what they were capable of. I wanted drivers who were disciplined, economical and thorough.

The trials were to take place over the test route every day for a month. It would require exceptional drivers.

For a start, every speed limit was to be rigorously observed. Whether on motorways, ordinary roads or through villages, towns and Manchester city. And that was not easy.

The driver had to be constantly checking and correcting his speed.

If there was a long drag in front of him he couldn't take a run at it if that meant exceeding the speed limit. Going downhill he couldn't let the truck coast. If it meant using the brakes to keep within the limit then he had to do so.

Each truck had a tachograph fitted – this was like an aircraft black box and monitored everything - and these were checked each night. The test had to be done the same way, day in, day out, for a whole month. The only change would be for the driver to swop vehicles every three days.

This was to prevent the human nature of the driver from thinking of the truck as 'his' truck and the competitiveness that might emerge.

It was tough, repetitive work and it needed a very disciplined driver. Not every truck driver could do it. I knew I could do it and I hoped Clive and John could do it as well.

Once the test started and the results started to come in, it was apparent that they could.

The different sections of the route showed up well on the tachograph. It was easy to see whether the trucks kept to the speed limits or not. They did.

The fuel results from the three trucks remained virtually the same no matter who was driving. Day in, day out, the results came in, were analysed and imputed into a graph. There were no sudden or unexpected jumps or discrepancies.

At the end of the trial the results were clear. Not what the customer wanted but clear and indisputable.

One of the competitor's truck returned the best fuel figure. It was only a half gallon difference over the daily route but that amounted to a lot of money over a year's driving in the real world.

It was back to the drawing board.

Six months later, we repeated the exercise with conditions as near identical as I could make them.

This time the customer's engine was the clear winner. The engine went into full production and, even today, is a well respected and reliable unit.

On the strength of those trials I got a lot of similar work. Clive and John took part in most of them although I got other similarly talented drivers in as and when needed.

We got an excellent name for ourselves as skilled and unbiased testers. And, just as importantly, we made a lot of money between us.

When I retired, I instantly recommended Clive as my replacement to my customers. They all agreed and he had been doing well out of development testing ever since.

So, that is the quick - Really? You call that quick? - version of how I met Clive Pindred. And, more importantly, just why he owed me a big favour.

So, back in my shed, the kettle came out yet again and we drank and remembered the good times.

We talked about John Slater, the other driver on that first road development test. A quietly spoken guy, he had been a very valuable addition to the team.

Sadly, John was no longer with us. He had paid the ultimate price for being such a great driver.

Three years ago, John Slater had deliberately crashed his own truck into the concrete support of a motorway bridge. It was either that or crash at full speed into a coach full of screaming schoolkids.

A wheel had come off the coach in front of John and he only had a split second to make a decision.

He chose the bridge, saved the kids and died instantly. A great driver and a very brave man who was still sorely missed.

Clive and I raised our cup to our fallen friend. We gave John Slater the traditional trucker's farewell. We wished him Good Roads and Far Horizons.

"I saw that article you wrote about John." Clive said quietly. "It was beautiful. I still get goosebumps when I remember his funeral and that convoy that accompanied him all the way from Kent to Coventry."

John Slater's body was placed on the back of a customised Kenworth truck and driven back to the crematorium at Coventry.

Throughout the journey he was leading a convoy of trucks that the police said exceeded five miles in length at one point.

It made the national and international news. I had the honour of planning that funeral and of driving the Kenworth truck. It was one of the proudest days of my life.

We both sat in quiet remembrance. Finally Clive asked what I wanted from him. I told him what, the reason and my plan.

He didn't hesitate for a heartbeat. "Just tell me when and I'll be there." He promised.

We spent a little time looking over the plot. He seemed quite taken. He said he envied my stress-free life but didn't think it was for him. I told him to wait a few years and see how he felt then.

I told him I would be in touch and walked him down to the gate. We shook and he climbed into his tatty looking truck.

It had been made to look deliberately tatty to avoid attracting any undue attention. Development work is very secretive stuff. The competition is always trying to get an idea of what any of their competitors are up to and will go to any lengths to do so.

A lot of development these days is carried out within the safety of a computer but nothing beats a proper real life trial carried out by proper real life people.

Clive told me that underneath all the grime on the tatty ERF was a very experimental hydrogen engine. One that was eventually going to revolutionise transport.

For a moment, I almost wished I was back in the game. But only for a moment.

I listened and smiled as Clive gave me a twin air horn blast as he drove up the road.

Truckers, eh? Salt of the earth.

Back in my shed, it took me quite a while to sort out the tumbling thoughts in my head. It had been an interesting morning.

I put my feet up and planned my planting list. Eventually though, I must have got distracted because the next thing I knew Jan Hawkn'spit was shaking my shoulder.

Chapter Twenty Two.

"How are you, you Plonker?" he asked. I looked up at him. I was feeling a little woolly-headed. With my eyes squinted, Jan looked a bit like Trigger in the Only Fools and Horses programme he was obsessed with. I guessed that I might have dropped off.

Shame, because in my mind, I had been driving my truck over the long bridge spanning the Mosel valley in Germany. One of the more spectacular views I carried in my memory. When the Seek and Find computer section of my brain was on track, that is.

Oh well, back to reality. I did think of yet another cuppa but was a bit awash with the stuff. "Hello Jan. How are you?"

"Cushty bro, cushty. I wanted to ask if you have any news on that tool sharing idea of yours? Only I have a contact for good stuff if you want some." Once a shopkeeper, always a shop keeper.

I told him that it didn't look like it was going to pan out. People had seemed very interested in my idea of a tool sharing co-operative initially then cooled.

It made sense, to me, to have a joint rotovator, quality strimmer or whatever was wanted rather than a lot of individuals all having the same tools.

But, once the nitty gritty details were brought up – where would they be stored, who would have first pick, what happened if someone left - people lost interest.

Jan liked the idea because he was used to co-operatives in his native Poland. Also because he wanted to make a bit of money on supplying some Stihl equipment he had a contact for.

He seemed a bit disappointed. I asked him how his other problem was doing. "Foo Kinell, those bollocking kids are doing my nuts in." he told me in his colourful English. Some of the other allotment guys thought it funny to teach him some phases that he thought were in common daily use.

"But, I am expecting a delivery next week so maybe you can tell your friends?"

I thought it best to keep quiet about The Allotmenteers and what we intended to do. I let him think that I knew people who could help him get rid of his problem.

The less people who knew the so-called vigilante group was really the only five of us decrepit Super Heroes, the better.

I told him I would pass the message on. I told him I would need the full details. Delivery day, whether the driver would play ball and where his next delivery afterwards would be. He promised to find out. He told me that the initial part of the plan had gone as well as I hoped it would. "His eyes nearly popped out when he saw them." Jan said.

As yet, my plan hadn't really been thought right through. It was up there percolating but not yet ready to serve up. I need to find out some other stuff about the problem before I was ready.

Right now though it was time to go home. Lynne wanted to go into town and had suggested that I go with her.

I use the word 'suggest' loosely. I guess I was going to be the muscle. She was going shopping for a 'little' pond. But, I suspected, there would be more involved than just a pond.

There would be sand to lay it in. Flat rocks to place artistically around it. A sandstone rockery would be in the background. Some paving slabs. It would involve a water pump for a fountain. Water plants to place decoratively in it.

Oh and not forgetting a large hole to place the preformed pond into. Guess who would be digging said hole? Don't be stupid. It would be me.

An old man with arthritic knees, painful shoulder joints, calloused hands and a pathetic fear of not digging said hole.

But, to be fair, I had been promising her a pond for years. I had finally got round to doing her decking.

I had also bought her a large summer house/artist studio where she would go to paint whenever the artistic mood took her. Sadly, the mood didn't visit so much just lately. I just wish it had stopped calling before I bought the studio.

The pond was way down on the To Do List. Or at least I thought it was.

But, either I had been very diligent in completing To Do List jobs or The Pond had mysteriously moved up the list. I couldn't remember being very diligent so I suspected the latter.

I love going shopping with Lynne. I am very organised and she isn't. It makes for an interesting time. I just love traipsing up and down Do It All's aisles, backwards and forwards, picking stuff up then going back to replace it and get something else.

But, many hours and two laden trollies later, we staggered out, blinking, into the spring sunlight.

It's nice spending someone else's money or so Lynne always tells me. I could have paid off the national debt of a small country with what we, correction I, spent on her 'just a little pond' and accessories.

However, on the plus side she did decide that, having been a good boy, I was in line for a special treat. I was thinking of something else but she was thinking more along the lines of a meal.

But she was paying so that was good. After loading everything into the party bus and tying the rest securely onto the roof rack I was ready for something to eat.

Fortunately, her favourite restaurant was just up the road. The old bus was groaning under its load but we eventually made it to our destination and parked up.

Judging by the number of cars, it looked to be pretty busy and we didn't have a reservation. But Lynne decided we would chance it anyway. As it happened, we were ok and got a table.

Half an hour later, we were finished. It was a good meal which we both enjoyed. Good company, for her, relaxing surroundings, and a reasonably quick service.

She had a 'healthy' McChicken burger meal and I had a huge Double Whopper Mcburger meal. Lynne had intended to pay but she couldn't find her purse and 'borrowed' my debit card once more.

I thought longingly of that bridge over the Mosel Valley in Germany and just how high it was. A person could quite easily fall off it if *she* wasn't careful.

The rest of the day was spent unloading the bus, marking out the pond site and surrounding area then digging a tentative first shovelful of rock hard earth. It damn near broke my wrist. The whole garden and she picked the one spot where the clay was the hardest and deepest.

I decided that enough was enough for today. She had waited this long, she could wait a little longer. I would make a start tomorrow. It might be softer then. Or not.

Inside, I phoned around and found that the cost of hiring a jack hammer and mini-digger was quite high. In light of the critical state of my debit card, I reluctantly abandoned that as an option.

I cooked our evening meal. Lynne lets me do this because I am a better cook and she prefers to spend her time more productively on Facethingy and Twatter.

Also because the ER doctor, after several visits, said it was probably safer.

Since my knee replacement operation, I had got into the habit of eating my meals standing up in the kitchen. Lynne gets waiter service and a tray on her knees in her room.

Using the kitchen like this gives me a chance to observe my neighbours. Lynne calls me 'The Neighbourhood Watcher' for some reason. Maybe the binoculars.

Because of the dual carriageway that separates us from our opposite neighbours, we don't know them that well.

And, of course, there is the perceived social status of their side of Victory Drive being higher than our side to contend with.

Of course, we say 'Good Morning Sir and Madam' bow and tug our forelocks when we meet but we don't socialise. Given that we don't know their surnames we have, for identification purposes, given them all nicknames. Nicknames that have, over the years, somehow stuck.

Mr Techno is always messing with gadgets like garage door openers and burglar alarms. The Gods are always going out Good Deeding and playing Cliff Richard cds. The Stallions are so named for the local landmark of a rampant horse painted on their garage door. The Greengrass' so called because he is always messing with his lawn.

What, you don't have nicknames for your neighbours?

The neighbours at the end of our garden we call The Glums because, well, because they are always miserable. We used to have a chat when we first moved in but it got so depressing talking to them that we now try to ignore them.

A bit difficult when they are always up at the bedroom window looking into our garden trying to catch a glimpse of me with my shirt off. It is becoming a bit of a pain being in the garden and having to suck in my stomach all the time.

They are the only people we know who never go on holidays or even a day out. Never, not once in the 31 years we have lived here. Strange people.

The guy next door has a used car lot and often parks his overfill vehicles in his garden and on the street. He's not so popular either.

So, what I am trying to say is that we don't really know our neighbours. Most of my friends are down the allotment. I don't think Lynne has any friends apart from me.

So it was a bit strange to see Mr Techno coming down our path as I was eating my meal. Perhaps he had smelt the liver and onion casserole? I was surprised that he wasn't armed or had security with him. It was brave of him to venture alone onto The Lower Side of the road.

Anyway, I went out to meet him and found out that he wanted to know if I had a copy of Word that he could download into his laptop. Apparently he knew I was an ex journalist and could therefore have a copy of the programme available.

Being an ex truck driver, salt of the earth, type, I sorted out a disc for him and escorted him safely back to his side of the road. I think he appreciated it.

Lynne had watched it all and thought I was being nice. Whether she was implying that I wasn't always nice or not was unclear. But, Mr Techno now owed me a favour and, some time in the future, I would call it in. It's nice when people owe you favours.

Women don't seem to grasp the principles of men favours. It is a bit like a sacred trust in that, once called upon to return a favour, you must do so immediately and, preferably, without whinging.

Chapter Twenty Three.

When it got dark I went out. I walked up to the old people home opposite the Downeybed shops. I hid in the car park and tried to give the impression that I was not lurking. A bit difficult when you are concealed in some bushes. Fortunately, it being almost eight o clock, the residents had retired for the night.

I wanted to observe the kids and try to get some information, some sense, of the hierarchy of the group. Obviously, as Linzi had told me, ET was the much older leader.

He was a thin, weedy looking youth with bad skin and an attempt at a moustache on his upper lip. He had long black hair under the hoodie on his head. He was dressed in the youth uniform of trainers, jeans , tee shirt and the almost obligatory hoodie.

But, he didn't appear to have any deputy or chain of command. He would give an order and the younger kids would obey.

I counted around ten of them. Sometimes more, sometimes less. Some went away but others joined the group. They were just milling around. Talking, smoking, drinking from cans and others were doing that disjointed stuff that passes for dancing these days.

The customers from the two shops and the chippy tried to ignore them. It was a bit difficult as they tended to get hassled both entering and leaving the shops.

One skinny little girl tried to lift the purse from a middle aged woman as she left the chippy with her arms full.

Quick as a flash, her hand was in and out of the woman's coat pocket. Just as quickly, the woman spun round and trapped the girl's hand between her body and the car door.

The girl shouted and squirmed but, in the end, just dropped the purse and pulled free. The woman gave her a kick up her skinny little bum, almost like swatting an annoying fly, and shouted something at her as she teetered away.

The other kids laughed and jeered the girl as she re-joined the group.

I watched for about half an hour. It was a bit bizarre. The kids treated their attempts to harass and steal from the customers as some sort of game.

The customers treated the kids as an annoyance rather than anything more serious. Other than a doing a bit of shouting, they seemed to accept the kids behaviour as normal.

It was a bit disconcerting to me, and any one of my generation I suppose, to see how things had changed.

As I watched I idly wondered just why and when things had gone so wrong. For someone brought up as a kid to treat adults with respect, just when had it come to this?

If I had tried anything like that at that age my parents would have clipped my ears if the customers or a copper hadn't done it first. Not that I would have been out at that time of night anyhow.

My kids had been brought up to respect people and their property and that was reflected in my grandkids behaviour. So, just when had it gone wrong? Sometime around the 80's I guessed.

Why was anyone's guess. Too liberal or just not bothered parents? Too many of the short, sharp knock rules being undermined by too many new liberal rules and namby-pamby regulations?

As I watched and pondered I began to wonder if it was worth my, or The Allotmenteers, time and effort to try to change things. But, I decided, it would be fun to try. And, at my age, any sort of fun is always a worth while pursuit.

*****

To ET, it was just another boring night. Out of the house with his mother not bothered or caring whether he was in or not. So long as she had her vodka and her fags she was quite happy staring at the tv all night.

When he returned it was more than likely she would be passed out on the sofa. Maybe he could get into her purse then. Pickings had been slim lately.

The Downeybed shoppers were getting too good at dealing with them. And the manager of the old fogeys home had stopped the wrinkleys from going across the road at night.

Instead, if they wanted anything, he would make up a list and send a worker over. And you did not mess with any of them. They'd clip you round the head as soon as look at you. Maybe dealing with the wrinkleys all day made them bad tempered?

Just as well some of his crew had brought some grub from home. They'd lit a fire down the rec and cooked sausages on sticks until they were either brown or black.

 The council wouldn't be too pleased when they saw the damage to the trees they'd got the wood from. Or the burnt grass.

He was going to have to do something different that was certain. He needed a big score to get some money and to keep his crew's respect. He'd already lost two of the bigger guys to the youth club the council had recently opened in town.

But, just recently he'd had an idea. A couple of days ago, he's seen the Pole shopkeeper get a delivery of stuff. A big foreign truck had pulled up right outside the shop.

The driver had opened the back doors on the trailer and started unloading. He'd been sitting in the bus shelter just up the road waiting to go into town. He'd got a good look inside the trailer when the driver was inside the shop. There were lots of pallets of what appeared to be food stuff.

But, it was when the Pole came out afterwards and the driver got back into the trailer that things got interesting.

The Pole was looking all around him as the driver reached behind some pallets and pulled some concealed boxes out.

The driver then handed over a box of what appeared to be vodka although it was spelt Wodka. Probably because the stupid foreigners couldn't spell. There was also a large carton of cigarettes passed over once the Pole had returned from putting the first box into his shop.

He could read Benson and Hedges on the carton. Cool. It looked like the Pole was selling smuggled booze and fags. Nothing wrong with that. Everyone had to have some sort of scam going, right?

But, what if he could get his hands on either a box of booze or fags? Somehow get them out of the trailer the next delivery? Maybe when the driver was inside the shop, he could get into the trailer and do a quick grab and away?

Maybe get some of his crew to distract the Pole and the driver? It was definitely worth thinking about. A box of booze or fags, maybe one of each, that would be something, wouldn't it?

How much cred would that give him? He got goosebumps imagining it. Yeah, he'd have to deffo think about that.

Meanwhile it was time to call it a night. You couldn't do much these nights as it got dark too quickly. Still cold as well.

The younger members of his crew were already whinging about the cold, missing Glee or some other stupid tv programme. Stupid little sods. Didn't they realise how lucky they were hanging out with him?

He thought about going into town by himself to do a bit of grab and run. Maybe a purse, a handbag or a phone. But that meant walking into town and he couldn't be arsed. Besides, there were so many cctv cameras about in Rugby these days it was getting riskier and riskier.

He knew that a police record or an ASBO would sharpen up his image but preferred to stay off the police or court's radar for the time being. If anyone was going to get caught, far better it was a crew member.

ET went home. He hadn't been missed.

Chapter Twenty Four.

My new bionic knees protested as I swung them out of bed at five thirty. Idly I wondered if I could somehow give them a squirt of my WD40 lubricant. It seemed to fix most things. Perhaps not.

The nice weather seemed to be holding as Zak and I walked down to the allotment. For some reason I found that my first cuppa tasted better down there. I brewed up and watched Zak as he raced round the allotment circuit.

There were plenty of rabbits about but they moved when he approached and resumed their feeding as he left. Soon there would be the good times for the rabbits coming along. Another reason why I paid particular attention to my perimeter fence.

I had thought of bringing my air rifle down with me but She Who Must Be Obeyed said it was cruel. Said person hadn't seen what the little buggers could do to a fresh crop of new vegetables.

I was the only idiot down there at silly o'clock. The air was cold but the morning mists seemed to have gone. I sipped my tea and idly went over the jobs I had yet to do. Not that many as I had already done most of my early preparation.

It was hard to envisage the allotment in another month as a hive of activity with almost feverish planting, potting out and pampering being carried out by sweaty tillers of the soil.

For now, I was as prepared as I could be. I had read the books, watched the programmes, consulted the oracles and sacrificed many pieces of colourful paper bearing my true Regent's head.

Bring it on. I was ready for the New Season.

Would this be the Season to be talked about in hushed tones of reverence and awe, I wondered as I sipped.

Could it compare to Seasons Past when the weather was perfect, the produce bountiful and of unbelievable dimensions?

Or would the seasoned tillers of the land spit and cross themselves when ever this coming 2015 Season was mentioned?

Like the Season of 2003 which is whispered about in terms of awe and terror. When the weather was so hot that everything scorched and burst in flames as it slowly and painfully emerged.

When water was rationed and the allotment was alive at night with furtive men, rustling raincoats and illicit watering.

When the old and revered allotmenteers were consulted on the best way to lift the curse of too much sun and not enough rain.

The wives of some of the more holistic soil shifters, it was rumoured, danced naked at midnight and performed indecent acts with sacred allotment tools in a vain bid to bring Nature's bounty of rain.

Peel away the skin of a modern allotmenteer and you peel back into centuries of myth, mischief and mayhem.

Distant tribal memories of failed crops and famine stretching back to Neanderthal times can unconsciously emerge from a stressed allotmenteer.

But, maybe this season would be ok. If not there was always the fallback plan. Aldi.

I returned home when I judged it to be safe. I had done all I could down on the allotment. I was the Man. As Zak and I walked home I mentally girded my loins. You should try it some time. It's sooo nice.

Hopefully Lynne would be up and that would relieve me of the stress of waking her. Thanks be to the Great Cliff, his music be exalted, she was up and eager to dig the hole for her pond. Or, to be more accurate, to supervise.

Unfortunately, as the first tentative shovel prodding revealed, the soil hadn't softened overnight. The shovel bounced back. Plan B. The Dreaded Pickaxe. The breaker of wrists and men.

Three hours later, with bruised and bleeding hands, broken back and tender feet, I proudly inspected the pond crater.

As I sweated, toiled and bled, I did idly consider going even deeper. Maybe to a nice even six feet? Then I remembered that the Glums and their constant watching made that idea difficult.

At around the same time I also remembered that I had sold THE COFFIN.

Yes, a coffin. I got it off Ebay a couple of years back. It had been used in one of the Dracula films, came with provenance, pictures and a penny pinching price.

I thought it was a good buy. I envisaged trying it out for size. Maybe putting in a little bookshelf, some sort of lighting, a decent music system. You know, getting it nice for whomever of us went first.

After getting it comfy I was going to store it in the garage. The Bride of Dracula had other ideas.

She didn't want it in or near the house for some reason. 'Over my dead body' was the firm and final threat.

It was a tempting offer and I had watched enough CSI to know I could probably get away with it. But, reluctantly, I decided to offer it to a similarly like minded, forward planning, individual.

Preferably single or with a friendlier more accommodating wife, partner or friend with benefits. It went back on Ebay.

There was a lot of frenzied bidding which I showed to Lynne to prove that I wasn't the only idiot out there. In the end it went to a lucky bidder down in Devon for a lot more than I paid for it.

I knew it was a good investment. Lynne agreed.

She spent her share –and mine- of the profit on a 'must have' crafting gizmo that would save her seconds of her valuable time.

The buyer contacted me to arrange collection. He seemed very keen.

The mutually agreed day arrived and Lynne worriedly called me into the kitchen to watch the arrival of the said purchaser and his companion.

Two Gothic visions in leather and latex, studded stuff and heavy boots clomped down the path. The one I thought was a male was small, stick thin with black eyeliner, deep red lips and a mohawk.

The other had jet black, badly dyed , hair, red contact lenses, - I hoped – a leather studded jacket and a fifties style Teddy girl swishy, multi-petticoated skirt and little black pumps at the end of tree trunk legs.

She, again I am guessing, must have been six foot three, and big boned enough that the house shook with each step. Her face was chalk white with black lipstick and badly smeared eyeliner.

After the big build up, they turned out to be very nice and ordinary. Friendly as well. Goes to show you can't go by appearances.

They didn't say what they wanted the coffin for and I didn't ask. Some images are best not imprinted in one's mind.

The guy cheerfully paid and I helped him carry it out to his vehicle. As we walked respectfully up the path, coffin on our shoulders, I couldn't help but notice the sea of semaphoring shades and blinking blinds from our High End neighbours.

I played to the crowd by pretending to slip as I exited the missing gate. There was a huge collective sigh as I managed to hang onto the coffin. I asked the guy to put it onto the wall for a minute to rest. He quickly picked up his cue and patted my shoulder. His companion re-smeared her mascara with her tissue dabbing.

I took off the lid and peered inside. I re-arranged my imaginary body, bent over for a last lingering kiss and replaced the lid. I got out my handkerchief, dabbed at my eyes and shook my shoulders. I turned my face to the heavens, waved a fist skywards and shouted "Why.. damn you… why?"

Solemnly we picked up our burden and carried on round the corner. There was no pretence at hiding now. Every curtain was drawn back, every blind split. We slowly approached his vehicle.

Now, to be fair, I was expecting something a little bigger. An mpv, an estate car or a van. Even a hearse maybe. But not a Ford Ka. That was a surprise. Idly I wondered if a sporty fuel injected version would be called a Ford Ka.Si. Maybe not.

I looked at the coffin. I looked at him. Finally I looked at the woman mountain. "Ummm" I thought. "This should prove interesting." It did.

It ended up with his girlfriend literally crammed into the lowered back seat. The front passenger seat was also lowered back as far as it could go and the tail gate opened as high as it would go.

To the incredulous stares of my High End neighbours we eventually slid the gleaming coffin into the car.

Well, most of it. Well, ok, about two thirds of it. I got a white cloth and hung it on the end of the sticky out bit.

I tied the tailgate firmly down. I watched as he somehow got into the driver's seat. He started up and moved off. He gave a cheerful little wave. She didn't. I don't think she could move anything.

As I watched the Ford Ka lopsidedly drive away I had the 'All the way to Devon?" final and incredulous thought. It does indeed take all sorts.

Dabbing at my eyes with my handkerchief, I waved until they were out of sight. Slowly and with great dignity, I returned to my supposedly now empty home. I saw a couple of my neighbours behind the glass with their mouths wide open. She was drying her eyes and looking sadly at me.

As I walked down the path, Lynne was looking daggers at me. Me and my weird sense of humour eh? It'll be the death of me, she keeps promising.

So, to recap, that was the reason that it was a preformed garden pool and not a coffin that went into the laboriously dug hole after first preparing it with a Saharan sized base of building sand.

Once that was properly tamped down the pond shell was lowered with due respect and dignity. The mountain of dug earth was artistically transformed into a rock garden.

This involved placing the rocks and boulders purchased yesterday into sympathetic positions and carefully, yet creatively, half burying them again.

A sprinkling of newly planted and pleasantly posed rock plants were cunningly concealed yet displayed in their crags and crannies.

Water plants, in little black baskets, were reverently sunk beneath the waves. A mournful bugler played Taps as they were laid into their final resting place. The Glums were in bits up at their window.

Finally, yes finally, the piece de resistance, the whole focal point, the hugely expensive solar panel powered water fountain was, after several location changes, up and furiously fountaining.

A celestial choir sang in the heavens above. Hallelujah! Lynne finally had her water feature installed and working. Job done.

Chapter Twenty Five.

After all that excitement we went in. I made tea and, together, we sat out on the decking and proudly studied and appreciated our water feature. At least, Lynne did.

I painfully studied my wrecked hands, blistered feet, felt my sore muscles and, strangely, didn't quite appreciate it to the same extent. Must be a man thing.

But, it must have made a huge dent in the To Do list. Nearly, I guessed, as big as the hole in my bank balance.

Maybe I would reconsider that tour of the Downeybed Prestigous Retirement Home for Retired Gentlefolk after all. It boasted a mature, carefully tended garden that was 'ideal for quiet and contemplation'. That was a definite plus in it's favour.

After such an exciting and productive day, my creative juices were spent. An old fashioned good long soak, a stiff shandy and a warm bed beckoned.

Tomorrow was another day. The odds were 50-50 I would get to see it. Getting old is such a rush isn't it?

I had my usual three hour sleep, four hours trying to sleep and the knowledge that the old guy with the scythe had passed me by yet again.

This morning was a repeat of yesterday's. We old folk like our routine. Everything in its place. Everything just so.

Sometimes to vary my routine or maybe as a test, Lynne will give me a different knife or a fork to eat my meal with. To overcome this little faux pas on her part, I have taken to hiding my cutlery after carefully and secretly marking them first.

Lynne says I have OCD. Obsessive Compulsion Disorder. OCD'ers like everything to be a certain way. We call it being neat and tidy in an obsessive way.

That is why my room is always neat and tidy with everything in a logical, easily reached position. For instance, my three remotes are arranged in length. My table mat is precisely aligned with the two corners of the table. Things out of alignment or logic tend to catch my eye.

I know that some people take OCD to extremes. Having to perform certain rituals in a precise and complex way before opening a door or switching off a light. They can't help it and the rituals reassure them. I haven't gone that far but I do like to do things in a certain way at and at a certain time sometimes as well.

The dogs get fed at four and, whilst they are feeding, I go upstairs and shut all the windows and curtains in preparation for the night. Things like that.

As I get older I tend to rely on these little rituals as a way of remembering to do other things. Fed the dogs, do the curtains. I don't find it odd but it annoys Lynne.

I tell her that she has OCD as well but hers is the reverse to mine. I like neatness and order. She prefers chaos.

When I am cooking, I tend to wash up and put away as I go. When Lynne cooks everything seems to come out. She will taste the gravy or stew using a spoon. That spoon gets laid down and another spoon get used for the next tasting. She never believes in using one item when twenty will do.

The kitchen mess was probably the reason why I now do all the cooking. When I came off the road, Lynne cooked and I washed up and cleaned up afterwards. A simple meal or a complex one, everything still got used. I did suggest a dishwasher but she said she already had one. She said I was old but still did a reasonable job.

Initially I did try to persuade her to wash and tidy as she went. "You do it your way. I'll do it mine." was the reply. She would make a quick egg and chips and I would be stuck in the kitchen for ages afterwards.

So that's my OCD out of the way. You now know that I an not perfect. Sorry to shatter your illusions but you had to know.

That is why I now cook and do most of the cleaning. I find it easier. On both of us.

It is the same down the allotment. Why I weed every time I go down. I find it easier to keep on top of things. Which is why my plot is always, you've guessed it, neat, tidy and weed free.

My neighbour, Adrian, is the same so with both of us hacking at the weeds daily, they don't grow, germinate and spread into neighbouring plots. Except for the Marestail that is.

That invasive weed has got into everyone's plot and there doesn't seem to be any cure. Weedkillers don't touch it. The roots go down so deep that you can never cut off enough root to kill it completely.

Both Adrian and I have found the only thing that temporarily halts its onward march is daily weeding. Keep cutting the root as far down as you can and this seems to weaken it and keep it under control.

But, this morning there was no sign of Adrian. Hopefully he was still down in Kent and sorting something positive out with Anya.

I asked Lynne once if, in a similar situation, she would tell me to get someone else. "Of course I would" she said brightly. "I was thinking of Angela for you".

Angela is one of her friends. One of those feisty women who is always protecting Women's Rights. She is bossy, demanding, high maintenance and not the best of lookers either. A bit horse faced with bad breath and a lazy eye. Not my first choice.

" I thought you didn't like her." I pointed out. Maybe she had hidden qualities. Like a large bank balance.

" I don't." Lynne replied cheerfully as she moved away. I thought she was laughing. It was a joke then. A joke, right? ….Right?

I did my usual five minute weeding. I got a bit distracted when Zak started chasing a Muntjac deer. There a few of these tiny deer around. Usually single although there are rumours of a little herd in the wooded area beyond the allotment boundary fence.

They are the size of a Labrador dog, dainty and secretive. They tend to come into the allotments at night to forage. The one Zac was warily chasing was a male with tiny horns. Last year he started chasing one which chased him back. Since then he was always a bit half hearted and quick to return to me at the first hint of aggression.

Pete came down the path and Zak used this as an excuse to forget the Muntjac and resume his duty guarding me. He's only small but, in his mind, he's a Rottweiler.

Pete didn't want a tea but was in a talkative mood. "I've been speaking to Adrian." He said as he pulled a chair out and sat down.

"He still down in Kent?" I asked as I got my tea and sat down along side him.

Pete chuckled. "Yeah. He said you practically ordered him down there. He told me to say thanks. Apparently it was the push he needed. She's a nice lady. I hope it works out for them." He turned to me with a puzzled look. " He also asked me to pass on another message. Perhaps you'll know what it means. He said you were wrong. The ladies love it white."

I explained. I then told him about the pond I had just finished. Which led to talk of graves which led to coffins.

 I told him about the Dracula's coffin episode. He laughed at the image of the Ford Ka, the coffin and the two Goths.

"Strange what fashions the youngsters wear these days. Full skirts and petticoats." He mused. "We used to see a lot of them in the fifties and sixties

 Girls dancing at the old Granada with their skirts and petticoats flying out. Showing their legs, suspender belts and sensible knickers." He looked over and we both grinned. Days of our youth. Long gone.

" Afterwards, outside, we would try to creep up the leg, past the nylons and onto the bare flesh with the suspender straps." He shivered at the memory. It was a cold morning so I shivered as well.

"We used to call them gigglers." I remembered with a laugh.

"Damn right" he said with a fond smile. "Do you remember why?"

In unison we both said "Because if you got that far, you were laughing."

Happy days. We returned to the present. There was some small talk about the allotment, who was planting what and why. How many empty plots there were and the likelihood of them being let.

Finally we got round to The Allotmenteers. Pete asked me how my little scheme was coming along. I told him I was planting some ideas in that particular area and expected to see some results. I told him about my surveillance work the other night.

"We have got to do something." I told him. "It's getting out of hand. I reckon we need one good short sharp shock to sort it."

I gave him the more general outlining of what I was proposing. He thought it out and made a couple of little suggestions. One of them was easy enough to implement. The other I would have find.

"No, you won't." he told me. "I have something in my garage that will do the trick. It won't even take that much modification. I'll drop it off later. If you're not here I'll stick it under…." He looked around… "that black pot over there by the greenhouse."

"Who are we letting in on it?" I asked. "The five of us or not?"

He considered. "Adrian… if he is back in time. We can use his posh accent. Big Mick because……..well because he's big. Paul and his tool box might be handy as well. So, all of us. I guess." He turned to me

"Have we got enough vehicles? I don't particularly want to use ours. Although Big Mick's probably won't be seen so that one is not a problem."

"Well, I had intended to use Big Mick's anyway. Plus the vehicle my mate is supplying alongside the Polish contribution, I reckon we are set. Jan said Tuesday or Wednesday day next week. But, until we know for sure, we can't make any final plans. Everything might change. I'll just play it by ear and see how it goes."

"And Jan doesn't know? Does he still think it is someone we know from outside the allotment?"

"He thinks it is some hard men we know. I won't disillusion him." I smiled at Pete.

Chapter Twenty Six

ET seemed to spend all his time just lately watching the shops. There was no sign of another foreign truck coming. All that came on a regular basis were bread delivery trucks. Sometimes a van with some packs of tinned food from a wholesaler.

He hadn't told any of his crew because he wanted to do it himself. He could already imagine the respect he would get when he began bringing bottles of booze to the nightly meetings at the Rec. Not to mention the fags. But, not too many. He had plans to sell on most of what he could nick.

That's all he wanted. One sizeable wedge of cash and he could buy something a lot stronger.

He'd smoked weed twice before and knew that the rest of the crew were curious. With the money from the ciggies and booze he was sure he could score a bag of grass which he could sell locally.

Keep the profits and buy a bigger bag. Making money wasn't that hard. Buy cheap. Sell high. Make money. He just needed the initial funding.

As he lounged against the computer shop window, he began to daydream. Nice clothes, nice cars. Flash the cash and the women would swarm around. Proper women. Not like that skinny Brittany or fat Tahita. Women with decent handfuls up top who knew how to treat a man properly.

As the daydreams got more hot and steamy he almost missed the Pole.

The lanky shopkeeper had come out of his shop and was talking to a customer. "Foo Kinell Bro, I won't have them till Thursday. You'll have to wait till then or just pay the proper price. Hokey Dokey?"

 He looked around to make sure there was no one in earshot. He either missed or just dismissed the kid leaning against the computer shop window as unimportant.

"My truck driver friends can only bring so much in at a time. If they get caught by the bollocking customs they lose the lot. They have to be careful. Yeah, the same price.

Polish Wodka is good eh? The Russians say they make the best but that's rubbish. We Poles have made the best for a long time." ET heard The Pole telling the guy.

The two of them laughed and shook hands. The other man moved off and the Pole called after him "Tell your friends. After Thursday, Yeah? Cushty bro, cushty."

Finally, ET thought. Thursday is the day. He had plans to make. Maybe it would be better to bring one or two of his crew on board. The biggest and the fastest. He mentally rehearsed his moves as he walked slowly home.

Wait until they are in the shop. Run up. Jump up, Find the goodies. Hand them over to his guys, Grab a box for himself. Down, Run off. Easy. What was so hard about that. Proper planning was the answer. What could go wrong?

Chapter Twenty Seven.

Nearly the end of another month. The day after tomorrow was April the First. It seemed the older you got the faster your time went. Another of Nature's little jokes.

You retire expecting to have time on your hands. The minute you do, Nature speeds up the Space Time Continuum's clock. Not for everyone. Just the old people.

The ones whose illness/complaint gets dramatically worse once regular work and exercise stops. The ones whose brain gets slower and slower and their hard drives get fuller and fuller.

The Twirlies waiting for the bus only to be told they are Too Early –Twirlie – and will have the wait for the next one which may be past the nine o' clock deadline for their Bus Passes to begin.

The Bingo-ers eyeing down with infinite patience as the bingo caller chants out Keys of the Door, Legs Eleven and similar magic numbers.

Not realising or perhaps, not caring that the nice young man calling out the numbers – Dear God, make it a big jackpot – is in fact counting them out of the Biggest Game of all. Life itself.

This year April had seemed to creep up on us. We tended to play a lot of tricks on each other down the allotment. Last year, four of the Allotmenteers went down in the evening and rotovated Big Mick's plot.

We tidied it up and planted a load of daffs - very cheap at Aldi's - in the ridges we had created.

We planted twelve cans of lager – cheap at Aldi – around his shed. We moved the current shed seat in and chucked out the battered milk crate Big Mick usually sat on.

We went up to the Gregg's shop the day before and asked if they knew Big Mick. Knew him? He was a legend.

We paid for a dozen of his favourite savouries and left a note to be handed over with the pastries when he came in, as he always did,   the next day.

And, if said purchased snacks could be prettied up with a nice box, serviette and little sauce sachets, it would be appreciated.

I handed over five McDonalds barbeque sauce sachets for the box. I doubted that Big Mick would even glance at the writing on them.

I had dummied up a letter from a pr firm purporting to be representing Greggs. In it the pr boss thanked Big Mick for all his loyalty and hard work in keeping Greggs in full time business.

And, on behalf of a grateful Greggs, its employees and the whole country, would he please accept this little token of their admiration and esteem?

The manager, who must also have had a warped sense of humour, quickly entered into the spirit of things. He promised an all staff line up to cheer and clap as the box and letter was handed over. He also said he would sort out a Greggs hat which all the staff would sign.

The youngest and prettiest employee would hand over a large bouquet of flowers and an equally large kiss.

I learnt later that money had to change hands before she would agree to this. Obviously she did indeed know Big Mick.

We got to the allotment around eight the next morning to watch Big Mick arrive. He was carrying a large box, wearing a white Greggs hat with writing on it and very red lip imprints on both cheeks.

He looked at his new chair, his magically appearing host of golden daffodils, his crop of lagers, his tidy allotment and, unexpectedly, his face scrunched up and tears began to run down his cheeks.
"This…..this… is…the..best. day of my life."
He sobbed.

Not exactly the April Fool reaction we had planned but, all in all, we were more than pleased with the outcome.

We didn't even mind that we were not invited to share in any of the pastries or cans that we had bought.

The problem now though was "What can we do this year?

With old White Hair fooling around with a Pole down in Kent, we were a man down. We had to keep it simple. Paul, Pete and I had a planning session to see what we could come up with.

In the end we printed off a template we had found on t'internet.

This was to make a paper envelope similar in size to a seed packet. Following the template guide, we made several of these packets individually printed with what looked like planting directions for exotic seeds. We made up names like Spaghetti Surprise, Macaroni Magic, Baked Bean Bonanza and Cheddar Cheese Cascades.

We particularly liked the Dunking Doughnuts and The Greggs Sausage Roll versions. We put old seeds we had lying around into ten of the finished seed packets and an accompanying note.

The note was purporting to come from a well known seed supply company. It read:

Dear Mr McAvoy.

Thank you so much for your kind and valued support last year.

We hope you had as much pleasure from planting, growing and enjoying the results from our seeds as we have had in supplying them to a man of your calibre.

In recognition of your support and, in appreciation of our esteem, we would like you to accept the enclosed seeds.

We have, due to the confidential nature of the seeds,   hand delivered them to your allotment to avoid any of the potential breakages or missing items problems which can sometimes occur with Royal Mail.

We must stress that the enclosed seeds are experimental and very confidential.

We have had great success with growing them in laboratory conditions and we would like you, and a few other of our selected customers, to continue the experiment under allotment conditions.

We would be grateful if you could keep a log of planting times, weather conditions and crop yield.

There should be minimal watering and fertilising for the best results. We recommend planting in ridges approximately five inches apart.

In the case of our latest experimental seeds, the Dunking Doughnuts and the Greggs Sausage Rolls, we recommend indoor planting and regular feedings of a diluted sugar and jam mix for best results.

One of our representatives will be in contact with you shortly in order to answer any questions you may have.

In appreciation of your efforts, and those of the other selected growers, we plan to give a prize of £1000.00 for the grower of the best results from this exciting new range of our seeds.

We wish you all the best in your endeavours and, finally, to remind you of the confidential nature of the tests.

Thanking you

Youve Ben Hadd.

Director of research.

We put the letter into an envelope and, along with the seeds, made up a nice sturdy boxed parcel. The plan was to place it in Big Mick's shed on the last day of March. Somehow we didn't think he would twig it was an April Fool's joke.

Who knows, it might even get him interested in actually growing something on his allotment.

I have no doubt that we would also play practical jokes on each other as well.

Silly things like putting superglue into padlocks. Or stretching cling film over shed entrances. Little trip wires to stumble over . Putting red vegetable dye into a water butt.

Last year, I made lots of little holes on Adrian's allotment.

I pushed a broom handle into the earth, built a little mound of fine earth around it and carefully removed the handle. Instant mole hills.

That one nearly drove Old White Hair mad. He even went out and bought some mole traps and set them.

Maybe even painting a shed or two a different colour? On second thoughts, maybe not.

I wouldn't be doing any practical jokes at home either. The fall-out from last year's selection is still firmly etched in my mind.

Who could guess that stretching cling film over the toilet bowl would fail to amuse?

Or a large fake furry spider placed on a door to fall onto the person opening it might not be seen as even slightly funny to an arachnophobic person?

And why would fake dog crap on a bed pillow cause anyone to throw a hissy fit?

Talk about not having a sense of humour.

It is hard to believe that it is nearly April already. A whole quarter of a year already passed. Where has the time gone since the extravagances of Christmas?

One minute you are just getting over the unaccustomed rich food fest, the next you are thinking of summer holidays.

Another few weeks and there will be potatoes to dig. We have already enjoyed the first crop of early new potatoes.

Soon everyone down the allotments will be in demand as the bringer home of fresh salad produce.

The hunter gatherer feeding his tribe regardless of the time, effort and personal risk involved.

Where men, brave men, can walk proudly home with their kills slung over their shoulders. Stride into their caves and, to the delight and awe of their dependents, unashamedly display their carrots, lettuce, tomatoes, radishes and other such hard fought for delights.

To announce that, once again, the harsh winter has been survived and now the good times are here again.

Eat family. Grow strong and plump with the produce that I, as your wise and daring leader, have provided with absolutely no danger to myself.

Build up your reserves of body fat in anticipation of the harsh winter yet to come.

When the allotment is dead and unproductive. Where the only thing between us and slow starvation is our stored food and the odd trip to Aldi.

Some of the guys on the allotment like the summer time the best. Probably because they can see and eat the results of their endeavours. The hard labour forgotten as they tuck in.

Others like the early spring when they can plan ahead, plant and experiment. Will borlotti beans be better or not? Less cauliflowers and sprouts in favour of new types of lettuce and green leaf salads? Be bold and experiment or be safe and stick to the tried and tested?

Then there are the ones who prefer the autumn when the hot summer is over and the growing cycle is slowing down.

When cabbages, cauliflowers, carrots, turnips and swedes come into their own.

When the onions are harvested, cleaned and stored. When the last of the late crop potatoes are dug, sorted and stored in preparation of the approaching winter.

When early mornings and late evenings have a nip in the air and bring the worry of whether it is worth while getting the fleece covers out or not.

Should the manure be ordered now and left in a pile to rot down over winter? Or, spread now and left to work its own way into the soil? Which is best?

Is it worth bothering with the allotment next year? Time to call it a day and spend more time with the family?

What is worse, time spent down here or queuing in Aldi?

I like all the seasons. But then I used to be a workaholic and dislike doing nothing.

For some reason, Lynne thought sitting down driving a truck all day was similar to doing the same at home whilst watching tv.

But, being a loner by preference, I do tend to lean towards the winter months down the allotment. The quiet of a winter morn as the snow, sleet and hail lash down.

The finger numbing frosts that cause you to always carry a lighter with you to heat up frozen padlocks. Using a hammer to get enough water to boil a kettle and having to melt a viewing patch on the ice laden shed window with your breath.

But then, get a cup of tea, the portable gas fire going and looking out over the white allotments is very peaceful and beautiful.

Even better if old White Hair came on down to spend a moment. I guess he gets lonely in his bungalow by himself so, when he sees me and Zak, he tends to walk down to borrow a cup of sugar or a spot of the grey and sludgy milk powder mixture.

On the road, my friends or acquaintances tended to be other truckers or the warehouse men I met. The only problem with that was my work very rarely involved regular collections and deliveries.

Sometimes I wouldn't see a driver or other guys I knew for weeks or months at a time.

It was only since retiring and getting this allotment that I had any regular contact with those I now called my friends.

Initially it had taken patience to get these shy allotmenteers to come out of their shells and trust me. Weeks of just a nod of the head that then led up to a 'Good Morning!'

It was 'The Troubles' as the Collins incident was referred to that brought the five of us together as a united team. Now, I felt like I had always known them.

Big Mick with his penchant for food and violence. A big guy with a good heart. At least for now.

Taciturn Paul with his mechanical and produce growing skills. The 'Go to guy' for tips and advice.

Pete with his passion for detail and his knowledge of locks and keys. A guy with a sense of humour like mine who is able to keep secrets between just the two of us.

Adrian, another loner like me, who had recognised a kindred spirit and reached out to me in his time of need. In his own imitable, white hair flaunting, 'shiny as a diamond in a dung heap' kind of way.

My mates and fellow Allotmenteers. If I didn't have the allotment then I would only have Lynne.

Keep the allotment then.

Chapter Twenty Eight

Jan Hawkn'spit had news. The delivery company had contacted him with the final delivery details. It would be in two days. The only problem was that, due to a heavier than normal schedule, the driver was unlikely to reach him until the late afternoon/ early evening. Would that be ok? Jan said it would be not only cushty but perfick.

As well as Only Fools and Horses, he was also a big fan of the Darling Buds of May re-runs. More because of Ma Larking/Pam Ferris than Mariette Larkin/ Catherine Zeta Jones. He preferred his women with a bit of meat on them.

He sometimes wondered if he should take a drive down to Pluckley in Kent to try to find them.

He had already tried to find the Trotters in Nelson Mandella House in Peckham but nobody seemed to know where they were. Perhaps they had moved somewhere else?

Maybe that detective Frost who looked like both Del Boy and Pa Larkin would know where they were. Could it be possible they were brothers or cousins?

It was difficult in England. Nobody seemed to know anybody. In Poland everyone knew each other and the family history.

The problem was that he had heard Detective Frost worked in Yorkshire and he wasn't quite sure where that was, other than that it was up North. He did know that they spoke English with a funny accent and he wouldn't be able to understand them.

He knew all this because Big Mick down the allotment had told him. Dave called him Big Mick but some of the others called him Lar de Ars. He didn't know why he had two different names.

But he did know that the big man was very helpful teaching him things about England. He told him all about the Trotters, the Larkins and the Frost and where they lived.

He was the one who taught him lots of good English words to use. Words like Bollocking and Foo Kinell. He used these words a lot in his shop and people liked to hear them. It made him feel proper English.

Big Mick had told him that up North there was a big wall that the Romans had built across the country. He said it was still there and it was to keep the North people and the Scottish people out of England.

It was called Adrian's Wall like the white haired friend of Dave's. The people on the other side weren't in the Common Market and so couldn't come over to work.

 He said it was no use going to Yorkshire to find Mr Frost because he needed a permit. And, even if he got the permit he wouldn't be able to understand the people because they didn't speak English very well.

Maybe Dave would know? He had to go an
see him anyway with the delivery news. And
to get the final part of the plan for getting rid
of those bollocking kids.

He decided to ask his wife to run the shop
while her went down the allotment to see if
Dave was there.

*****

ET saw the Pole leaving his shop. He
watched as he walked down the road towards
him. ET was in his bedroom watching the
road outside on his tv.

He and five of his crew had gone to the big
Junction One shopping area on the Leicester
road. Whilst the others made a nuisance of
themselves in Maplins, he had lifted a little
cctv camera from a display stand and walked
out with it.

The staff were too busy watching his crew to
bother about him. Now he had the camera
poking out of his bedroom window and was
watching the shops in comfort.

He guessed that there was another delivery
due soon. The shop was always busy so it
needed to get fresh stock in.

He hadn't been to school in days because he
was afraid of missing the delivery truck. His
mum hadn't said anything so he guessed she
didn't know or wasn't bothered.

She didn't seem to know much about anything these days. She slept in late and then spent the rest of the day watching the tv, drinking vodka and smoking fags. He thought she might be taking something else she was so spaced out sometimes. He had looked around one afternoon when she had gone to the post office for her money but hadn't found anything. Whatever she was spending the money on it wasn't food.

There was hardly anything in the house to eat that wasn't stale, growing mould or long out of date. If it wasn't for his crew bringing him food he'd be hungry.

But, if his plan worked, he'd have a bit of cash soon. He intended to use that cash to buy a few E's and start dealing. Using the cash and profit from one deal to buy an even more gear the next time. Within a year, he'd be been rolling in money.

Provided, of course, his start up fund in the shape of a delivery truck, turned up with the goods.

He got up and watched the Pole as he walked down the road. He was probably going to the allotments at the end of the road. He'd seen him walking back sometimes with bags of green stuff to sell in his shop.

Wouldn't it be funny if he was growing cannabis down on the allotment? Maybe not as he knew you needed lots of heat to grow the stuff. But an allotment? That was just for the old wrinkleys wasn't it?

Chapter Twenty Nine

I was feeling very old as I put my tools away. Pete and I had decided to give Adrian's plot a bit of a dig over on the spare patch beside his spuds.

Not knowing how long he'd be down in Kent gallivanting, we thought we'd make a start on his plot for him. It had turned out to be a bit of a race as we both tried to outdo each other.

Not making it noticeable of course but it did get very competitive towards the end. With shovels flashing in the sunlight and a fine mist of earth in the air around us, we both dug furiously.

He reached the end first but he'd cheated. He had been digging bigger shovelfuls than me and more of them.

But I was a good loser so that counted for something, didn't it? An acting award if nothing else.

Now my new knees were aching as they creaked dryly. I bet Steve Austin didn't have to put up with any of this dry joint rubbish on his bionics.

Sometimes I wondered if they really were new. Maybe they had been recycled or previously owned as the posh term for second-hand now is.

The NHS was all about cost saving so why not save on kneecaps? Maybe my knees weren't really new but had a few thousand miles on them already.

That would explain why my walking posture had changed so much since they had been fitted. I used to walk with a nice even wear on my heels. Now, as evidenced by my uneven sloping heel wear, I was walking differently.

I used to have a nice jaunty young man walk now I was shuffling along like a pensioner. Aah. That might explain it.

I was just about to go home for a nice long soak when Jan called my name as he walked up the path.

"The delivery is in two days" he told me excitedly. "In the afternoon or evening. Is that ok? It will be on a Friday." He told me unnecessarily. He didn't have to explain things like I was a doddery old man.

"And the driver knows he has to contact you first?" I asked.

"Yah, yah. I left message he has to phone first. He will get message."

"Right, then I will be round later on this evening. I'll park round the back. You'll have everything ready?"

"Yes." He assured me. "Everything is ready." His face clouded over a bit. "I will get them back, yes?"

"Probably. It depends on how well you do your part. I'll do my part, don't worry. The people I am dealing with are ready. You just phone me when the driver has called. You know what to say to the driver?"

Jan assured me he did. There didn't seem much else to say so I told him I would see him later. If he had any other questions, he was to ask me then.

The nice long soak had to wait. Lynne wanted me to go shopping at Aldi for a 'few' things.

I had only been let go shopping by myself since last year. Before then I had to watch and learn the finer points. Every now and then I was allowed to do a dummy run at the local shops before the real thing.

Then I was allowed my first real 'big' shop. Armed only with a list, a purse and a stout heart, I entered Aldi.

Actually I like Aldi because I used to shop with them all the time when I was on regular German runs. I do like cheap stuff.

It must have gone well because when I returned home, battered and bruised but beaming with pride, I was even allowed to 'put the stuff away' in the sacred sanctum of the larder.

I could get used to this man lib malarkey. I didn't have a bra to burn but, if I did, I definitely would.

Although lately Lynne does keep saying that I really should consider one. Personally I think she is jealous that my 'moobs' are bigger than her boobs.

Anyway I get up to Aldi in Lynne's car and park up. I get lucky and get a spot near the doors. I locked up, located a trolley – using my newly acquired token – and prepared to do battle.

As soon as I got inside I knew there would be trouble and tears. They'd done the unthinkable and bloody well moved everything around.

Now my OCD and I like routine. I like to go straight to everything on my list with the least possible distraction and distance. I have often been complimented on my technique. Not that one, the shopping one.

People say it is like watching poetry in motion as I accelerate smoothly through the customer chicanes.

Weaving and watching as my prey comes into site. A quick grab and, with hardly a break, onto the next item.

Bypassing stuff that isn't on the list, I move at speed through the throngs of lookers. I ignore the special offers, the BOGOFF's and the Once they're gone, they're gone, traps for the unwary and inexperienced.

Like a local know his roads, I use all the rat runs as I fight against the flow of less skilled shoppers. I can lift stuff from the shelves with scarcely a break. Spot my tins from over an aisle away.

I push firmly but gently against the 'stop in the middle of the aisle for a chatters'. The old ladies who weave drunkenly side to side – almost as if they are deliberately trying to block you – the ditherers and the taker backers who leave their trolley slap bang in the fast lane. I take no prisoners nor stop to chat in my quest for a 'good' shop.

But, today, all was lost. Everything had been moved to different locations. I would have to memorise my routes once again. No longer a Supershopper but back in the ranks of the newbies, the occasional and the lost. It was a total disaster.

Eventually, many frustrations, bruises and weird looks later, I had the final hurdle fixed firmly in sights. Everything on the list secured or equivalented. No item left behind to forever shame me. I had nearly completed my task.

It is an unwritten rule in supermarkets that, the busier they are, the less tills are available. Of the six possibilities in front of me, only two were manned. I scanned the queues, established who was on the tills and, based on past experience, ran the permutations and possibilities.

Kevin, the nice but slow, against Misery Mabel. With the former you could have a nice chat but would be better off with a chair to sit on as he painstakingly performed his till duty.

Mabel didn't chat, didn't smile but moved things along at speed. Her arthritic hands were a blur as she pushed items past the scanner. If an item didn't come up, she knew the price without having to ask someone to find the item to check.

I had just decided to go with Kevin when a husband and wife team with double trollies spotted his smaller queue and swooped.

I reluctantly joined Mabel's and weighed up the odds of finishing first. I reckoned with a couple of 'no prices' I could just nose ahead and put the upstarts in their place. A single shopper against a duo. It had been done before.

I was just catching my breath and getting Lynne's purse ready when I had a moment of déjà vu.

I thought I recognised the guy in front of me. Could it be? Was it possible? It was. Geoffrey Leighton-Bradbury in the flesh. Talk about a flashback.

My mind flashed back to that fateful Aldi shop last year when I was behind a High Side neighbour I recognised.

It was Geoffrey and we got talking whilst waiting for a woman to find her purse. During the course of that conversation it transpired that he had an allotment.

I had no interest in an allotment until he mentioned that IT GOT HIM OUT OF THE HOUSE. That part I was interested in.

I hadn't been retired that long and was getting under the Boss's feet. It was around the time of my Second Unaccompanied Big Shop.

Getting an allotment suddenly seemed like a brilliant idea. I asked if there were any vacancies and was told there weren't but 'there might be a way round' method of bypassing the waiting list.

That was how I got my allotment which used to be Geoff's. He moved away with his gardener girlfriend, now his wife, and I moved into his allotment.

Now , here he was in front of me again. I tapped him on the shoulder. He turned round, eyed me up and down and was preparing to turn round again when he finally recognised me.

He was just up for the day and getting a couple of bottles of wine for a barbeque at his new young wife's parents place.

 He asked after the allotment and I told him the full Collins, murder, mayhem story.

 Almost before we knew it we were through Mabel's checkout and free.

I sneaked a quick look over at Kevin's till and was gratified to see that the dynamic duo were still not finished. I gave him a 'Hard luck, old chap' look which he reluctantly acknowledged. To the victor, the spoils.

Geoff had mellowed somewhat. Before he had been an 'up his own bum' type of bloke. Now he looked younger, more relaxed and chatty. We chatted for a while, catching up then parted with a lot of 'nice to see you again's' and 'come down the allotment anytime's'.

 It wasn't that nice and he probably wouldn't but it would have been satisfying to show him round MY allotment this time.

Back home I recounted my shopping disaster to Lynne as I put the stuff away. She didn't seem that impressed or even very interested.

'Now you know what I used to go through' was her final verdict. Some days you just can't win.

After my hectic shop I needed to unwind but couldn't. Tomorrow was a Thursday and Lynne did her White Glove house inspection on a Thursday.

Actually she did it on any day of the week ending in 'day' but Thursday was the official one.

 My OCD and I liked to keep things nice and tidy. I vacuumed every day and dusted every other day. Because I was a man I could multi-task and breathe as I dusted.

I don't panic about the inspections anymore. I keep a tidy house.

But I did sometimes sleep on the floor the night before inspection. This avoided messing up my army style, tight as a drum, bed. Doing this saved time the next morning. Time better utilised on a last minute panic dust around. I wish I had my Brave pills again.

Usually I passed. The times I didn't I would run naked round the garden. Lynne didn't make me. I just liked doing it. Usually to the surprise and delight of the ever vigilant Glums.

Eventually, I was finished. Shopping and dusting completed. A man's work is never done but this old man was done in.

But, first I had to go up the shops for a little collection. It didn't take long and I was back home again ten minutes later.

We had a nice healthy salad for tea. I love salad or so I am told. We seem to have a lot of them.

Then the delight of a long, hot, soak. An experience that a shower cannot even come close to replicating. Pink skinned and glowing I watched the tv for a while and, around eleven, called it a night.

I decided I would sleep on the bed tonight after all. I needed a good night's sleep.

After yet another sleepless night of tossing and turning, I got up at silly o'clock again and had another quick dustaround.

To my relief I passed yet another inspection. I suspect that Lynne only did them to ensure I didn't slack in my househusbandly duties.

Sometimes I almost wished that I was a woman and could spend my time frivolously on Facethingy or Twatter.

Oddly for England, it was raining quite hard outside. No point in going down to the allotment as there was nothing urgent. I decided to go over my plans for tomorrow.

I rang Clive Pindred and gave him the news. He said it fitted in nicely with his plans so that was ok. I did have an alternative but it wasn't quite as good.

For the moment though, things looked ok. Any last minute changes or hitches would have to be sorted out tomorrow.

Siesta time beckoned. I whistled up the dogs. They would guard me and keep me safe whilst I siesta'd.

I got up suitably refreshed an hour later when the heat of the mid-day sun had diminished. Made a cuppa and mentally reviewed my plans.

Unfortunately, the mid-day sun had only lasted an hour.

Outside it was still raining that soft kind of Midland rain. But so much better than t'hard rain you got up the always wet and windy North.

I don't like being inactive so decided to go down the allotment anyway. I took Big Mick's seed box with me to save me going down again later.

 The chances of him being there were minimal. Lottery winning minimal.

There was no one down there at all. I placed the box in Big Mick's shed which was easy to do with no door. I placed it at the end of his two seater where no one else could see it but he just might.

I heard the main gate squeaking and saw Pete plodding up the path. I wondered what he was doing but guessed when he saw me and smiled.

 "Great minds think alike" he said "I thought I would take advantage of the rain as well. Have you left it?"

"Yes, it's at the end of his settee. What did you have planned?"

"I thought I might do something for Paul." He grinned as he pulled something out of his pocket. We went to Paul's shed and I watched as he very quickly picked Paul's lock with the lock pick in his hand. It was a good quality padlock but an expert like Pete could open it in under a minute.

"I thought we could put all his tools in Adrian's garage." He suggested.

"Yeah, good idea but we don't have the key to the gar....oh..." I said as the penny dropped. We didn't need a key. We had a Pete instead. Did you know thieves and safebreakers used to be called Petermen?

We quickly gathered all Paul's hand tools and went up the path between my allotment and old White Hair's.

He had a gate from his garden straight into his plot. Handy. His garage door lock proved no more of an obstacle than Paul's padlock. We put all the tools inside and Pete quickly locked it up again.

Back at Paul's, we moved his other stuff around. Tipped over his chair and generally made it look like a break-in. Paul wouldn't be happy. He loved his hand tools. Many of them had been passed down from his granddad to his dad and then to him.

He was always boasting about the quality of them. "You just don't get this type of quality today." He insisted. "All this foreign rubbish coming in. Take this hoe"

He would hold up his battered hoe. "This used to be my granddad's. He bought it new when he used to tend the gardens at Althorp House. " he told us yet again.

Althorp is the nearby Earl of Spencer's humble little residence and Princess Diana's final resting place. She is buried on an island in the middle of a lake.

"That was over a hundred years ago. And, apart from three new handles and two new heads, it's exactly the same." He insisted.

He wouldn't be best pleased to come to work tomorrow morning and find it gone then, we reckoned.

We left his shed door wide open and left some exaggeratedly big footprints in the mud for him to find as clues. They were simple to make. Place your foot down firmly and then wiggle it from side to side. You end up with some impressive prints.

Satisfied with our efforts, we were wet enough to go home.

I walked through the spinney and opened the back gate. I closed it again and walked quietly back. Sure enough there was Pete just going into my shed. Give him his due, he was quick.

I watched and waited. When he came out he looked all around. Satisfied, he walked back down and through the main gate. I gave him a few minutes, left my hiding place, and walked back to my shed.

Inside I found he had poured water into my sugar tin to solidify the contents.

All my tea bags had been emptied loose into the jar. The water in the container, when I poured a little out, was brown from the ground coffee inside.

The gas container had been unscrewed just enough to stop the gas coming out.

I screwed it back. I left everything as it was. I'd bring fresh supplies down tomorrow.

Just outside my gate a glint of metal caught my eye. Intrigued I bent down and, with a smile, picked up Pete's lock picks in their little plastic wallet.

I haven't picked a lock before but I had watched a master and he had often told me the mechanics of it.

 Back at his shed, I inserted a flat pick with a slightly rounded head into his padlock and pushed it all the way in. This pushed back the main barrel pin. Using a slimmer pick, I inserted it and turned until I felt resistance.

Levering upwards, I pushed the pin upwards and did the same for the next four. When all five were clear, I gave the main pick a final push and the lock sprang open. Was I good or what?

I did the same to his tea making supplies and used real ground instead of coffee to colour his water.

 Using one of the screwdrivers from his cupboard, I unscrewed the supports from his seat base. The next time he sat in it he'd get a real surprise.

 I closed the door, snapped the padlock shut and made my way back to my shed. I dropped the picks where I found them, hid in the spinney and waited again.

Sure enough, I heard the main gate opening ten or so minutes later. I had a job not to laugh as I watched Pete coming up the path searching for his picks. I had guessed he would go to put them away as soon as he got back home.

When he realised he'd dropped them, I knew he'd go straight back for them.

Not just because he didn't want to spoil his surprise but because they were valuable to him and he didn't want them ending up in the wrong hands.

I could almost feel his relief when he picked them up from outside my shed. He went home a much happier man still thinking he'd got away with it. As if.

I might not drive trucks much anymore and am getting on a bit but that doesn't make me a stupid old trucker.

I was looking forward to tomorrow and this year's batch of April Fool jokes.

Chapter Thirty

April Fool's day dawned brightly and, as usual for me, early.

After last year's painful retribution, I had decided against any major pranks against my ever loving wife.

My NHS supply of Brave Pills had run out and I couldn't afford to buy them on the street. So without my chemical courage, I decided on discretion and chickened out.

I did change her computer password but that was all.

She always has problems with her passwords so my little act of defiance would probably go unblamed.

It might even earn me some brownie points as I can make a big deal about going into the depths of my computer and resetting her password.

I am not supposed to know her password but, as she keeps it written on a piece of paper stuck to the back of her monitor, it is not too hard to figure out. She always forgets where she put the reminder.

To save long winded explanations, I just tell her that the little man inside her pc case is having a bad day.

I personally had often wondered about how a computer worked so I asked my older grandson to elaborate.

He explained about the little people who were specially bred for working inside computers. They sort out all the problems and daily tasks and work 24/7 if necessary.

Problems occur when they get sick or old. Once they are treated or replaced then everything runs smoothly again.

He knows a lot about computers does my grandson. I am lucky to have his expertise.

Armed with this technical knowhow, I am getting more confident and much better working with computers.

I was always worried that everything was being controlled by electronics and I knew that these were always going wrong.

Having a single little person in charge makes sense to me. I call my little engineer Fred and we seem to work well together.

I explain these complicated matters to Lynne as simply as I can. She accepts my expertise in these matters unquestioningly.

I sorted out some fresh supplies to make up for what Peter had ruined and went down to the allotments.

I knew that Big Mick always visited his shed around 7.30. This was after his night shift and after his daily visit to Greggs.

He lived for his allotment and the privacy it afforded as he indulged himself.

He chose to ignore the fact that, with no door, his shed and his habits were not private. But, wisely, everyone who went past when he was eating pretended that he was invisible.

I unlocked my shed and replaced my ruined drink making supplies. I grabbed a water container and made my way past his shed in my pretend errand of fetching water. I was just in time.

He had just finished eating and was cramming the remains of his Gregg's bag into his mouth. He is convinced that, because the contents were so nutritional, then the grease that leeched into the paper bag made that equally protein rich.

He mumbled "Morning" as I came into view. I pretended to be surprised that anyone else was earlier than I was.

"Have you seen Paul?" were his next words. He sounded a bit clearer as the remains of the sodden pieces of bag joined the rest of his breakfast. He pointed to Paul's shed with its door hanging forlornly open. " He isn't going to be pleased to see his shed has been broken into. Looks like it has been stripped."

I walked back to the next plot and looked into Paul's bare shed with its open door.

"It was like that when I came." He explained. " I didn't touch anything. Don't go too close. Forensics will want to go over it, won't they?" He drew my attention to the footprints clearly etched into the mud.

"Who ever did it was a big bugger." He
pointed. "Look at the size of his feet. If the
rest of him is as big there should be a drag
mark between the footprints." He joked.

"Bugger me. You're right. He must be big.
I'm surprised he didn't just pick up the shed
and walk off with it."

The sound of the main gate instinctively drew
our attention. It was an old habit going back
to the Collins era.

If the gate squealed and Collins came through
then everyone went immediately into safety
mode. The hinges were deliberately left
unoiled as an early warning system.

Of course it wasn't Collins. No one knew
where he was. He had just disappeared.

Instead it was Pete and Paul with a couple of
the other plot holders.

They carried onto their plots whilst the two
P's walked up towards us.

"Don't tell him." Big Mick whispered
urgently. "Perhaps he won't notice."

" What the bloody hell has happened to my
shed." Paul shouted as he broke into an old
man half run/half shuffle. He quickly looked
inside "All my bloody tools have gone." He
said in disbelief.

He glared at Big Mick. "Have you been borrowing them again?" he asked. Then he looked at the door. "Bloody hell, you've broken in as well. I bloody locked that before I left yesterday. What have I told you about borrowing my tools?" he shouted at Big Mick.

"They came down from my grand dad to my dad and then to me. They're quality items not like the tat you get today. They're antiques and irreplaceable."

"Calm down Paul." Pete tried to keep a straight face. "Maybe there is an innocent explanation. Why don't I put the kettle on and we can have brew and a think about it."

Pete's shed is four plots down so we all trooped after him. He unlocked his padlock and went in.

He quickly came out again. "Bloody 'ell." He said. "I forgot to bring a new gas can down. I'm out." He looked across to me. "We'll have to go to yours."

"Ok, I've got plenty of gas." I agreed. We carried onto my pad.

I made a big show of finding my key and unlocking the door.

I reached inside and grabbed the chairs. I handed them over.

"Make yourselves comfortable whilst I brew up."

Pete's face was a picture when I emerged five minutes later with two mugs of tea. He obviously hadn't noticed that I had carried a water container down with me. I went back to fetch the others, sat down and started to sip.

"Best cup of the day." I said appreciatively. Big Mick and Paul agreed whilst Pete was suspiciously sniffing at his mug. "Have you had anything pinched?" I asked Big Mick.

He considered as he swallowed. He must have an asbestos throat. "I dunno. I haven't really looked."

Which, given the empty nature of his shed, was probably not the best comment on his observational skills.

"Perhaps you better had while we finish our brew." I suggested as I sipped delicately from my Best Granddad in the World mug. It was obviously a correct statement. The mug part especially. "We can't all drink as fast as you."

He ambled off. Paul meanwhile was putting two and two together. As was Pete. "It was you two bastards, wasn't it?" Paul asked. Closely followed by Pete's "How did you know?" I grinned at them both.

"Yes." I told Paul. "But, it was Pete's idea." I added quickly. I looked at Pete." I guessed you would double back so I watched from the end of the spinney. Nice try."

"Bastards." Paul said although his mouth did twitch slightly. "Where did you put them?" He looked over at Pete. " I forget sometimes what you used to do for a living." He looked at me.

"Adrian's garage." I told him. " Nice and safe. Pete's idea again."

He nodded satisfied. He looked at Pete then back to me. "What did he do to you?"

"He put water in my sugar, emptied my teabags and put my coffee into my water container. He then unscrewed my gas canister so it wouldn't work."

Pete was nodding proudly until he remembered it hadn't worked. His face clouded over as he thought of something else. "What have you done to me?" He asked anxiously.

"I tried to get into your shed but, short of breaking the lock, couldn't do anything." I told him with an unseen wink at Paul. "Don't worry though, I'll think of something." I assured him.

Pete looked at Big Mick coming down with a box in his hand. He shouted up. "Hey, have a look at my shed as you go past. Make sure the padlock is ok and there is no damage to the door."

Big Mick retraced his steps two plots and looked. He returned to us. "Naw, I couldn't see any damage. But, guess what, there was this box in my shed. It was at the end of the chair. That's why I didn't notice it at first. Everything else is ok though." He reassured us.

He sat down on my chair which creaked in protest. He looked at his parcel.

"There are no stamps on it." He confirmed. He looked at it again. "That means it must have been hand delivered." he pointed out. " I wonder how they got in?"

"Well, is it addressed to anyone?" Pete asked him.

Big Mick's mouth moved as he slowly read the writing on the box. "It's addressed to me." He looked up. "But it doesn't say who it's from."

He slowly opened it and reached inside. His hand came out with seed packets in them. " Just some bloody seeds." He complained. "Hang on. There's a letter as well." He looked at it then handed it over to Paul. "Here, see if you can make it out. The writing's terrible."

Paul read the typed letter out aloud. There was silence as he finished. The three of us looked down as Big Mick digested the letter's contents.

" I wonder why they choose me?" He asked. "I don't even like Dunking Donuts. They get soggy and fall into pieces.

I wouldn't mind giving the Greggs seeds a go though. It would be nice to be able to grow my own."

He considered again. "Some of these other seeds look alright as well. I think I'll try some of those. See how I get on. I wouldn't mind that £1000.00 prize either."

He looked across at us. We somehow kept our faces straight.

He studied us then decided. "Can you give me some advice on the right way to plant them? Look after them and all that?" He asked Paul.

Pete and I suddenly had coughing fits. Paul was made of sterner stuff. "Ok. But you have to keep it a secret as the letter says. No broadcasting it." He squeaked.

Big Mick considered this advice.

"Yeah, you're right. Best keep it quiet eh? Thanks Paul. You're a good mate. You all are. When they're ripe, we'll all have some, right? A private tasting just between us."

We all agreed and pointed out that Adrian should be included. Big Mick agreed. "One for All and All for one." He said. "The Allotmenters." He held up his big hand for a high five.

We high five'd him with watering eyes and lots of coughing.

We chatted for another few minutes. Mainly about planting techniques and how big an area Big Mick would have to dig and cultivate. He was getting quite excited.

As we broke up he asked Pete if he could borrow a spade. He said he would get him one as soon as we retrieved Paul's tools.

It didn't take Pete long to perform his magic although, after yesterday, I wasn't quite so impressed this time.

We gathered up Paul's precious heirlooms and carefully carried them back to their now less than stately home. He fussed over them. Wiping them down and inspecting them for any damage.

Pete went to get Big Mick his spade. I watched him unlock his padlock. No reaction. I walked back to my plot, took the chairs in and washed the mugs.

I looked up the path. Pete came back from giving Big Mick his shovel and returned to his shed.

Big Mick was furiously digging. It looked like a JCB at work.

There were huge chunks of earth flying about as, for the first time in a long time, Big Mick's plot slowly turned from overgrown weed green to dark dug earth. It was mesmerising to watch.

Less than five minutes later I heard Pete shouting …. " You bastard. Oh, you bloody bastard." Next minute he's outside shaking his fist and a chair at me. I waved back.

One to me, I think. I love April Fool's Day.

*****

"He hasn't got any in at the moment. But he says he is expecting some around four this afternoon when he gets a delivery truck from Poland."

ET's ears pricked up he heard one of his neighbours talking to another. He looked out his bedroom window.

It was the skank from three doors up talking to her next door neighbour. Sometimes he quite fancied the scanky one. She was quite fit. Pity she was so old though. She must be nearly thirty.

"My old man had got a taste for his Bockwurst. He says they are a quality sausage." The skank continued.

"Those the big ones? The other asked. " I quite like a big one myself."

"Oh, we all know that feeling." The skank squealed. They both laughed.

"Stupid randy old women." ET thought as he closed the window. "Four o'clock, eh? I better get myself sorted. Get some of my crew together."

Ten minutes later he put down his mobile. Only one bothering to pick up and he wasn't available this afternoon.

Some stupid excuse about a doctor's appointment after school. He'd left messages for the others. They'd better get in touch soon.

But he already knew that mobiles weren't allowed in school so it was unlikely they wouldn't get his message until they came out of school. And that might be too late.

He wondered if he could pull it off himself. Grab a case of vodka and a few cartons of fags then leg it. He was fit and fast.

He worked out for at least five minutes a day on the exercise machines the council had put up around the recreation ground. Usually to an appreciative crowd.

He knew he could outrun the Pole and the driver. They were both old. But, could he do it carrying booze and fags?

Could he hide the stuff nearby and come back for it later? Would he have time? He really needed some help. He started punching the numbers again.

*****

"Hello?" Jan finally heard Dave's voice. There was no reply from his mobile number so he tried the landline.

"Ello you plonker. It is Jan. I have just heard from the driver. Luvely Jubbly. He will be in the place we agreed about three thirty. He'll wait a half an hour but then he must go. Is everything cushty?"

"Hi, Jan. Yes, should be no problem. Any sign of him or is he still watching the shop with his camera?"

"I know he is around and not at school. I saw him earlier.

Good job you spotted his camera poking out his window and guessed what it was for. I guess he will know when the truck pulls up, yah?"

"Ok Jan. I'll get there a bit earlier and get things sorted. When you are unloading don't make it too obvious what you are doing. We won't get to many chances at this. See you later, yes?"

"Foo Kinell Dave, what do you think I am? A stupid Polack? See you later." Jan put the phone down with a satisfied smile on his face. He hoped it all went well and he finally got rid of those bollocking kids.

"Clive? Dave. A5 truck stop around 3.30ish ok? Oh good. I'll be there about the same time to give you a hand. What do you mean, you cheeky sod? What zimmer frame?

Chapter Thirty One.

Et felt apprehensive as he saw the truck stopping outside the Pole's shop. He watched as the driver got out and went into the shop. He came out a few minutes later followed by the Pole.

ET got off his bed feeling slightly queasy. He hadn't been able to get any help and, now the moment was here, he wasn't looking forward to it.

He was seriously thinking of bottling out until he thought of what could happen if he got away with it. Still struggling with the Should I/Shouldn't I argument he decided there was no harm in having a look.

He hurried out pulling on his hood as he walked up towards the shop. He studied the dirty brown truck as he approached it.

He wouldn't fancy travelling very far in it. It looked a right old mess. The box trailer didn't look much better.

Both truck and trailer were filthy and run down. Probably because Poland was a poor country and the truck owners couldn't afford anything better?

No wonder they all wanted to work over here. What with the Social money, free housing and free medical treatment they were far better off in the UK. He's heard his mum sounding off about the foreigners enough times to know why they all preferred England.

Acting casual, he walked past the truck as if going to the bus stop. Once past it, he stopped to look in the computer shop window. Still acting casual, he looked back at the truck. It's rear doors were open and there was a pile of boxes on two pallets waiting to be unloaded.

He waited and then saw the driver and the Pole come out, each grab a box off the opened pallet and walk back into the shop. He looked at the computer shop clock over the counter and checked the time.

It was just over five minutes before they came back with two empty boxes. That explained the delay. They were obviously unpacking and stacking as they went.

He watched as they threw the empty boxes inside and the Pole pulled out a pack of fags and offered the driver one. Both lit up and inhaled deeply. They relaxed against the trailer and began chatting away.

Obviously they weren't in a hurry. He made up his mind. When they took the next boxes out he was going for it.

He wiped his sweaty palms down the legs of his jeans. Planned his moves in his head. No hesitation.

Walk up to the trailer, climb in quickly, find the booze and fags and get out carrying as much as he could.

His legs started to tremble as he watched and waited. Finally they ground out their fags, turned back to the trailer, hauled out a carton from the pallet and walked away.

Before he even realised it he was walking towards the trailer. Looked quickly inside the shop as he passed the open door. Nobody in sight. He put his hands on the trailer floor and levered himself up into the trailer and then over the pallets.

Inside, the floor was covered in empty boxes that had been thrown over the pallets by the door.

He quickly examined them looking for the booze or the fags. He was convinced they would be there.

There were plenty of boxes but they all looked the same. He'd have to sort through them.

With one quick look towards the shop he made his way deeper inside the trailer. He got onto his hands and knees so he was out of sight and to read the labels more easily.

He heard voices and quickly lay flat behind the cartons. He waited with his heart beating so loudly he was sure the men outside would hear it. He hoped they couldn't see him.

He tried not to picture what would happen if they did.

The angry shouts as they saw him and caught him. The arrival of the police. The arrest. The questions and then the charges.

If he was lucky he would get an ASBO.

At the back of his mind, a little voice told him that an ASBO would be good and give him a lot of street cred.

He lay as flat as he could get and tried to control his heavy breathing. The two men continued to chat as they approached. Good. That meant they hadn't seen him.

He had already decided to get out as soon as they left with another carton. He couldn't see anything resembling vodka or wodka and there certainly weren't any cigarette cartons. The whole thing had been a waste of time.

He heard boxes being pulled across the floor. Then, suddenly the inside of the trailer seemed to get darker and darker. Within the space of a few seconds, it had gone from light to this near dark.

It took him several seconds to realise what had happened. The doors had been shut. He was trapped inside.

He was just going to start shouting when he stopped. Thought for a minute. There were more boxes on board so they were going to be delivered somewhere else. Rather than attract attention now and almost certainly get caught, he should wait.

Wait until the truck stopped again and try to jump out when they started to unload. He could take them by surprise if he jumped out quickly enough. They wouldn't be expecting someone to suddenly emerge from the back of the trailer and run off.

Before he could decide to shout or stay, he felt the trailer sway slightly and then heard an engine start up. Almost instantly, the truck started moving and gathering speed.

No point in shouting now. He was trapped. He felt sick. Where the hell was he going to end up? And just how was he going to get home without any money?

And, he found out as he tapped his back pocket…no mobile. It must have come out as he jumped up into the trailer. He thought he heard something at the time but was more concerned with getting out of sight.

Well, he'd got out of sight, all right. Now was it a risk that he'd be out of mind, as well? He tried to think just who would miss him first. His crew? Eventually. His Mum? The chances of that happening soon were remote. The school? He didn't go often enough to be missed.

In the back of the fast moving trailer, in the strange twilight that filtered through the grimy roof panel, ET suddenly realised that he was alone and that no one would miss him. It was both a frightening and a depressing realisation.

He suddenly had the urge to burst into tears. No longer big and macho, the crew leader, he became a frightened boy. Frightened like some of the youngsters and the old folk he had bullied and stolen from.

Was this what it was like to be bullied and scared, he wondered. He supposed it must be. He knew that he didn't like it. He sat down among the empty boxes strewn of the floor and hugged his knees. And, despite himself, the tears began to flow.

Time passed as he remained in this strange trance like position and state. How much time? He didn't know. Didn't care. All he felt was the wind vibrations, traffic noise and road bumps as the truck pulled the trailer towards its next destination.

He was dimly aware of other vehicles passing, being passed but couldn't see anything and only hear muffled sounds.

He could feel the vehicle slow down, stop, then start off again. He was aware that it was cornering as his weight shifted and he had to hang onto the side rails. That had lasted for about half an hour.

Since the last slow down and turn, the forward motion had been stable and the noise from the tyres almost hypnotic.

The road surface felt smoother with less jolts and bumps. ET guessed he was on a motorway. Going in which direction, he didn't have a clue.

He could have been going north or south on the M1. Or North on the M6 through Coventry and Birmingham. Further than that his geography was a bit sketchy.

He hoped the driver wasn't returning home to Poland. There were still the remains of the two pallets in the trailer.

But, did that mean they were going to be delivered somewhere in England? Or were they damaged goods or returns that the Pole was buying on the cheap? Was he, in fact, on his way to Poland?

Surely the trailer would be inspected in Dover or what ever port before going on the ship? Maybe the driver was heading towards the Eurotunnel?

He remembered seeing bits on the telly about trucks and cars just driving onto special vehicle carriages.

There didn't seem to any inspections going on before the trains were speeding through the tunnel and ending up in France. Or was it Italy?

Was it possible there were no Customs inspection if a truck was going out of the UK and not coming in?

He worried at the thought. The Customs tried to stop drugs and illegal immigrants coming into England didn't they?

Why would they be bothered if drugs and illegal immigrants were being smuggled out of the country?

With a sinking heart, ET realised that there was probably no reason for anybody to inspect an empty trailer leaving England. That, within the space of 24 hours, he could be well into Europe.

Then what? The driver wouldn't be best pleased to find he had a stowaway. And if he already knew that he was on board, because he saw him trying to steal from his trailer, that would mean his abduction was deliberate. And......what would that mean?

Et suddenly realised that he could be in more serious trouble than he had thought. That it might not be just a simple matter of jumping out when the trailer doors were opened and running off.

That, if the driver already knew he was on board, then he would be ready to deal with him as he opened the doors.

More than likely there would be more than just the driver to contend with. ET didn't like where his thought process was taking him. If they were expecting him, what did they intend to do with him once they caught him?

Suddenly, he didn't want to think about that anymore. He tried to think of positive things but couldn't.

 All he could think about was what was going to happen to him once the trailer doors were eventually opened?

Then, almost as if his mind had decided to shut down, he fell into a deep sleep amongst the boxes on the trailer floor.

Chapter Thirty Two.

"Hello? Is that Dave? Hello mate…it's Adrian. Um…. I'm ringing to tell you that Anya and I are engaged…..Yes, I know it was fast work but you were right.

Time is too short…. Yes, she was surprised when I turned up. But, when I told her what you said, she agreed.

No, not straight away, I had to work my charm on her first…what do you mean, what charm? It's the white hair mate….does it everytime. You should try it sometime. Oh…of course…you can't…..yours is just boring grey isn't it?

Anyway, we still have a few things to work out but I thought you'd like to know that you were right to nag me….no it doesn't mean you are always right.

Anya sends a kiss by the way and to say …. Hang on…. I've got it written down. It's spelt DZIEKUJE. Je-koon-yeh. It means Thank you in Polish.

Oh,….you already knew that?

What?..... Say what?.. Is it dirty? It sounds dirty…You sure?....Ok….I'll tell her. Dave says Gratuluje Zareczyn…Is it? It means what?...Really? Ok I'll tell him. ….Anya says thank you and your accent was very good by the way….I've got it on speaker phone, that's how….

….You're a clever sod, aren't you?
Anyway….thanks mate…see you soon.
Take care."

I put the phone down feeling really pleased. I
knew he just needed a push. Everyone
deserved a little happiness in their life. I was
just going out to tell Lynne when the phone
rang again.

"Dave?..... Pete. Have you heard? Adrian
has only gone and got engaged, hasn't he?

You already knew?.....When?.....Oh, must
have been just before he phoned me
then….What?....No, he wanted to ask if I
could feed his fish and keep an eye on the
place. Well….. I asked him for how long and
that's when he told me.

Yes…I think it's great news.

By the way, I've just come back from the
allotment. You'll never guess…….well,
try……..oh, ok……Big Mick is still down
there digging away.

Says he's going to get all his seeds planted in
one big push. Well. He's not doing it just for
fun, is he……Of course he believes it. Well,
have you ever seen him doing any real work?

I just hope he has a good sense of humour. If
he finds out it was just an April Fool's joke
he might not be best pleased. Well…he's
going to guess, isn't he? He'll know it was
one or all of us.

By the way…..how's that other business
coming along?

He did?...when?.... Well, when are you gong to let him out? That long?...won't he be missed?

You sure? Oh well, you know best. If it was me, I wouldn't leave it too long. In the morning?...You're taking who? Jan?... what for?

....uh-huh. Yes I suppose.....you devious devil. Yeah, it will be interesting to find out. Ok, see you tomorrow....best of luck....good news about Adrian, isn't it?....see you."

I put the phone down once again. Thought about what Pete had said about Big Mick. Naw...he wouldn't...would he?

I went into the kitchen to make a cuppa. Lynne was there. I told her the good news about Adrian and Anya.

She burst into tears and went into the garden. "I'll bring your tea outside then?" I asked. What was she crying about? Just because Old White Hair was engaged or something else? Were they happy tears or sad ones?

 Why would she be unhappy about Adrian getting married? Her life was already complete. She had me. The perfect man. What more could she possibly want?

Chapter Thirty Three.

It was the cold that woke him. There was condensation dripping off the metal sides and roof of the trailer. There just the faintest of light glimmering through the translucent roof strip.

ET realised that he must have fallen asleep sometime during the night. He also realised that his bladder was bursting and that he was also cold, hungry and scared.

He stood up slowly feeling the stiffness in his legs. He had made a shelter from the empty cartons. He could feel the trailer moving and hear traffic noise so he knew he was still moving. Had the truck been going all night? And, where was he going?

But, first things first. He looked around for some sort of container. Nothing.

He climbed over the pallets and, hanging onto the side rails, tried to pee through the gap in the rear doors. The yellow stream ran under the pallets and down the floor channels. He didn't care. What else could they do to him?

He looked at the pallets hoping to see something to eat. He tore at the wrapping and, after some effort, managed to get a box out.

He tore it open and saw that it was full of currants or something in plastic bags. Taking a bag out he pulled it apart and took out a few of the contents. They looked like currants although the label said it contained Porzeczka, what ever that was.

He took a tentative bite and chewed. They were currants. He used to take handfuls when his mother was baking.

He was only little then and his mum hadn't done much baking just lately. He remembered the taste though. It made him feel a little homesick.

With his immediate hunger satisfied he looked for something to drink. He opened several cartons before he found one with tins inside. He looked at the label. Gruszki. What the hell was that? He shook the tin and heard liquid sloshing.

He hit the tin hard against the floor and only managed to put a dent in it.

Looking around he could see nothing with which to puncture or open the tin. He put it back on the floor and stamped on it. It rolled away and he lost his footing and fell heavily.

Lying there on the floor, he could see under one of the pallets. He noticed a bit of wood, more a large splinter, coming from one of the pallet slats.

He reached out and, after a lot of effort, pulled it free.

He stood up brandishing his makeshift tin opener and felt the wetness on his legs. He'd been lying in his own pee. He didn't really care. He had more immediate needs.

Standing the tin up, he stabbed at it with the sharp end of the splinter. The flimsy point just bent. He broke off the end until it was a bit more substantial and tried again.

This time it dented the lid. He stabbed harder and felt the point go into the lid and something going into his hand as well.

He looked down and saw a sliver of wood had broken off and gone into his hand.

Blood was flowing onto the tin. He grabbed the splinter and pulled it free. Shaking his hand to get rid of the blood, he examined the damage.

There seemed more blood than anything. He put his hand to his mouth and sucked. The salty taste filled his mouth.

Once he had finished sucking, he looked at the wound. Just a little hole and nothing serious. He pressed the cut against his trouser leg and pulled it away once he felt the acidic stinging from his own urine.

He remembered the tin and picked it up with his good hand. He shook it and was rewarded with a spurt of liquid from the hole he's managed to make. He tested the liquid with his finger and a cautious dabbing tongue.

 Once again a familiar taste came flooding in to transport him back home once again. This time to afternoon tea with pears and evaporated milk. Greedily he raised the can and, with difficulty, drained the syrup from the pears it contained.

With hunger and thirst satisfied for now, he began to take stock of his more immediate situation. Stuck in a trailer, going God knows where and no way of getting out until the truck stopped and someone opened the trailer doors.

It didn't look very good.

Even as he contemplated his situation he felt the motion of the trailer change. He thought he sensed a change in the noise as well. A few more minutes and he was certain. The truck was not on the motorway anymore. It was definitely going slower.

With more trepidation than elation he waited to see what was happening.

If the truck stopped would he be able to get away? Once the doors were opened , how much time would he have to get out before anyone realised what was happening?

Even as he tried to plan, he felt the truck coming to a gradual halt. The sudden absence of traffic and wind noise inside the trailer was disconcerting.

It was like background noise that had suddenly been turned off. The silence really was deafening.

He'd heard the phase but never knew what it meant. He did now. Even more so as he realised that the truck's engine had been turned off as well. He heard the truck door slam and the nothing.

His heart was pounding and he felt sick. The heavy syrup from the pears came back into his mouth and he swallowed it back down with difficulty.

His mouth was suddenly dry and his whole being was focused on the trailer doors.

Was this it? Were the doors going to be opened? Would he have a chance to get away? And, where the hell was he?

With mixed emotions he heard noises from outside the dors. It sounded like dry metal being freed. Then there was a bang as though something had dropped down.

Slowly a hand appeared in the ever widening crack and weak sunlight crept into the trailer.

He quickly retreated back into the trailer with legs that were suddenly shaking. His eyes drawn once again to the slowly opening door.

He saw his discarded makeshift can opener on the floor and quickly picked it up. Holding it against his chest he waited. He was struggling to breath and he could feel his rapidly beating heart. A singing noise filled his head and he felt faint.

Finally the door was thrown fully open and he could see a large man shape silhouetted against the weak sun. He could hear something being said which he couldn't understand and could hardly hear because of the blood rushing in his head.

The shape spoke again "Hey!" it said angrily.
Very angrily. "Was zumn teufel machts du in
meinem trailer, du kleiner bastard?".

When he didn't speak, the voice spoke again
in halting English. "Hey, what are you doing
in my trailer you little bastard?"

Finally he managed to reply. "Nothing mister,
honest. I got in here by mistake. I haven't
taken anything, honest." He croaked licking
his dry lips.

The shape drew back and then hauled itself
into the trailer.

Before his eyes it materialised into a very tall,
very large man with a mop of fiery red hair.
Red hair sprouted from the neck of his
stained tee shirt.

He looked around and spoke again. "you say
you take nothing? But I see empty paketer
und beschadigte dosen....Scheisse, was is
dast Englisch?...empty paketer and damaged
tins....Who pays for this? I must talk to my
boss."

Without another word, the man jumped out of
the trailer and closed the door.

ET didn't know whether to be glad or afraid
as he found himself on his own again in the
dark.

Chapter Thirty Four.

I went round to Jan Hawkn'spit's shop. He was waiting. "Hallo, Boss. You have news? Is everything cushty?"

"Morning, Jan. Yeah, everything seems to be working out fine. My friend Clive rang a little while ago. He is putting the final bits into place. We need to be there in about half an hour. We will go in my friend's van. He said he will be here soon. Is that ok for you?"

"No problemo, Boss. Luvely Jubbly. You want a coffee?"

"Yes, a quick one. One sugar."

"Hokey dokey, one cuppa jarva coming upsidaisy." Jan assured me. He really needs to broaden his viewing habits.

Like most continentals, Jan or his wife, made excellent coffee.

 In England, I had tried hard to replicate the taste of the coffee I used to enjoy on the continent but only succeeded when I started using evaporated milk from Aldi.

It wasn't the coffee, it was the milk that gave it that distinctive smoky flavour.

When I was on the road, I used to drink gallons of coffee and smoke countless cigarettes. At that time, I was around nine stone and had a twenty eight inch waist. I'm not and don't anymore.

I gave up smoking, after a tortuous and mammoth effort, six years, five months, three days and seven hours ago. Not that I'm counting or anything. Even now I sometimes sidle up to a smoker and try to inhale some second hand smoke. I reckon it must be like being an alcoholic. You always want one and you can never have just the one.

The coffee addiction I replaced mainly with tea although I still like a cup of coffee around eleven. Jan's coffee was still much better than what I make for myself. I must get the recipe from him one day.

With the coffee finished, we went round the back and waited. It was five minutes later that Big Mick's battered van came round the back of the shops.

It was Big Mick's day off so I wasn't worried about him missing sleep or anything. I had already told him that he would be paid for his fuel and time. I had thought of promising him some Gregg vouchers but decided he could make that decision himself.

I already felt bad enough about all the digging and planting he had been doing. I didn't want the thought that I was encouraging him to eat himself to a heart attack on my conscience.

I told him where we were going and we set off. It wouldn't take long. I just hoped it was all worth it.

Fifteen minutes later, we had arrived at our destination. And, from what we saw when we pulled up, we were just in time.

Chapter Thirty Five.

ET finally heard the sound he had been dreading. The sound of the door bolts was terrifying. He had been waiting for around fifteen minutes in the near darkness.

Outside he could hear vehicles drive up, stop, start up and drive away again. He didn't know where he was only that there were a lot of trucks about and it seemed busy. He just hoped it wasn't a port.

He had pretty much given up the idea of escaping from the trailer once the doors were opened. There didn't seem much hope of getting away with it.

The red haired giant knew he was inside and wasn't very happy about the damage he's caused.

It was only a few packets and one tin, he reminded himself. Hardly the crime of the century. And, he also reminded himself, not the booze and fags he was hoping for.

He had realised very early on that there was no vodka or cigarettes. The incident he witnessed must have been a one-off.

Strangely, he wasn't that bothered about his get rich quick scheme anymore. He was more concerned with getting away and that didn't look very likely.

The door opened and the shape appeared again. "Come here, boy." The man said in a voice that didn't expect refusal.

"I'm sorry mister." ET stammered. " I didn't mean any harm. I'll pay for any damage. Just let me go and I'll send it to you, I promise."

"What? You think I am stupid? I have spoken to my boss and he says to either get payment now or bring you back with me to Poland. There you can work for him until you have paid for the damage."

"I can't go to Poland, mister. I've got school. People will miss me and".. here a sudden thought gave ET an idea..... "Besides, I've got no passport. So you can't take me. I will need a passport to leave England." he explained.

"Scheisse, you need no passport. The stupid English Custom men don't search trucks leaving England. For why would they? So boy, what is it to be? You pay me now or come with me to my home."

ET eyes grew wide with fear. Why didn't the stupid guy understand? He had no money and didn't have much hope of getting any.

"I haven't got any money, mister. Honest. I'm still at school. My mum hasn't got any either. She is sick and I'm the one who looks after her. She relies on me. If I'm not there, she will probably starve to death. And that will be murder. You've got to let me go" He pleaded.

The driver seemed to consider. "Ok." He said finally. ET's hopes rose then were dashed again. "You must come mit mir, with me, to Poland. You tell my boss, yes? Maybe he let you make telephone call."

"No, no mister. Please. Just let me go. I won't say anything." ET pleaded.

The man didn't say anything. He just beckoned ET towards the back of the trailer. His whole attitude told ET not to mess him about. He knew that if he didn't go voluntarily, the man would come in after him. At least outside, someone might see him and call the police.

"I'm coming, mister. Don't hurt me please." He whimpered as he slowly made his way towards the open door. The red haired man seemed to fill the door space.

Just as he reached the end of the trailer, the man's hands shot out and grabbed his ankles. Holding on firmly, he pulled the struggling ET out of the trailer and onto the ground. Quickly releasing his grip, he grabbed the boy's shoulder.

ET felt his fingers digging in and knew he had no chance of breaking free. He squirmed half heartedly but knew it was no use. He was caught. Now, what was going to happen?

Chapter Thirty Six.

Just as we pulled up we saw a big red haired man dragging something out of a trailer. It turned out to be ET, the leader of the Downeybed shop gang.

But this was a different ET. Where before he was usually cocky and full of himself, this time he looked scared stiff. The big guy hauled him out of the trailer, set him on his feet and clamped two big hands on his shoulder. We could see him frantically squirming.

Big Mick blew his horn and we got out. The big guy looked at us. "Clear away. This is not your business." He snarled.

"Let the boy go." Jan told him. "Otherwise it will be bad for you."

"You?" The redhead laughed. "You think you can scare me." He shook ET firmly.

"This boy try to steal from me. He damage my load. He must pay."

ET shook his head in disbelief. He looked around. They were at some sort of truck stop. There were lots of trucks around.

He shook his head in bewilderment. That was the Pole from the shops. What was he doing here? And the wrinkly whose tyres he had slashed was here as well

What were they doing here and who was the other big fat guy? Were they here to rescue him? His hopes soared.

"Let him go and I will pay you for the damage." Jan said. "Come back to my shop with me now and I will pay you. Or the next time you deliver to me. Give him to me or we will take him."

"Nein, you will try to take him. You will not." The redhead promised. He took one hand off the boy, clenched his fist and shook it at the three men.

Without another word, The Pole launched himself at the big trucker. ET realised he was free as the trucker let him go and turn towards the Pole. He pulled quickly away.

He bumped into something soft, turned in terror and saw that he had crashed into the old wrinkly.

He felt the old guy pulling him away and towards the van. The fat guy, the driver, was standing by the open side door and reaching for him.

Looking over his shoulder, he saw the Pole and the redheaded trucker swinging at each other.

The Pole might be tall and thin but he was really hammering away at the big truckdriver.

The other was giving ground. Then, just as he was being pulled into the van, he saw the trucker take a fist right onto his jaw, stagger and then go down hard.

The Pole stood over him with his fists at the ready but it was all over. The truckdriver just lay there and seemed out for the count.

He watched as the Pole gave the drive an almighty kick in the ribs and then walk back to the van. He looked in at ET and quietly yet breathlessly asked "Are you ok, boss?"

Without another word ET threw himself at him and wrapped his arms around him. He buried his face in the Pole's chest and his shoulders started to shake as the tension left him.

Jan looked down at him and then, hesitantly, patted his back.

He just stood there until the boy stopped crying. He held out a handkerchief to him and watched as he dried his eyes.

"Come on boss. Time we got you home. Okey dokey. Luvely Jubbly."

He fished a bottle of water out of his coat pocket. He also pulled out a little bottle of pills and took one out. "Here boy." He said as he handed them over. "Drink and an aspro. It'll help you."

ET didn't need any encouragement. He put the pill in his mouth and drank greedily from the bottle. He got quietly into the van and they drove off. Out of the back window, he saw the big driver still laying flat out on the ground.

He looked at the Pole, the wrinkly and the big fat driver. "Thank you." was all he managed to get out before the van was speeding up the road.

His eyes were suddenly heavy and he couldn't keep them open. Within minutes he had fallen into a deep sleep as the relief at being rescued overtook him.

When he next opened his eyes, he was still in the van but it wasn't moving. It was dark outside though.

How long had he been out and, more importantly, where was he?

Almost fearfully, he got up from the bench seat he'd been sleeping on and looked out of the front window.

Suddenly he recognised where he was. He was at the back of the Downeybed shops. He was home.

Almost as if he'd been watching and waiting for him to wake up, the Pole approached the van and drew back the door. "Allo, sleepy head." He smiled. " How are you, boss? Cushty? Do you want something to eat or are you going to go home?"

ET knew there was no point in going home to get something to eat. There wouldn't be much in the pantry and he was starving.

"Is it ok if I have something here?" he asked hesitantly. "I'll pay you back when I get some money."

"Sure bro, no probs." The Pole agreed. "Come on in and we'll talk about paying me back. And, not just me. There is also my oppo Dave to pay back as well."

"Dave? Who is he? Is he the fat guy? The van driver?"

"Naw, Dave is the old guy whose car tyres you slashed. He is also the man who telephoned all his truck driving buds to keep a watch out for the truck you were in." The Pole told him.

"You were lucky. He got a phone call to say the truck was spotted on the M1 near the M25 junction.

He guessed that the driver was going to Dover and then home."

They walked into the back of the shop and ET sat down as the shopkeeper made him a drink and a sandwich before he continued.

"We got into the van and drove pretty damn speedy down the motorway. We arrived at the last service station before Dover just as the driver was pulling you out of the trailer. You were a pretty damn lucky bugger."

ET could only nod his head. His mouth was full of the best sandwich he had ever tasted. He nodded as the Pole asked if he wanted another.

"I put it on your bill, boy." He laughed. "Pretty big bill now. How you going to pay?"

"I don't know, but I'll think of something Mister." ET promised as he ate yet another large sandwich.

"You don't call me mister." Jan told him. You call me Jan or Boss. While you sleep in van, we think of way for you to pay us back."

"Anything. I'll do anything." ET promised him before being told what he had to do. By then it was too late.

Strangely, he wasn't too unhappy with the deal.

Chapter Thirty Seven

We were back at the Red Lion in Crick. Yesterday had been a hectic day for Big Mick, Jan and me. A long and tiring one. We needed a break.

I had asked the others if it was all right for Jan to join us. They said it was ok this one time but Big Mick said he wasn't joining the gang. I think it was Jan's promise to buy the drinks that swung it.

Adrian had joined me for his usual cuppa in my shed this morning. He had driven home last night. He was full of plans for Anya and himself.

It had been decided that she would sell up down in Kent and move up to Rugby when her house was sold.

I think the thought of being with old White Hair and near her daughter's memorial garden had been pretty much a foregone conclusion.

I gathered that a decision as to whether she would move into Adrian's bungalow or purchase a bigger place together was still being discussed jointly.

Selling a large detached house down in Kent would certainly realise a very healthy sum of money and buy something nice in the Rugby area.

But, for the moment, she was staying down there and getting things sorted. They were planning to get married in two months time. They didn't want to wait, he said.

He also asked if I would be his best man. I told him there was no argument. I was obviously the better man. I told him it would be an honour and a privilege for him to have me as his best man.

Show Anya what she could have had.

I tried to persuade him that some Grecian 2000 would take years off him but he didn't agree.

 Great, that meant that I and my dull grey hair and white face would be competing against his shiny white locks and his deep tan at the altar.

Oh well, it would upset Lynne seeing the contrast between the two of us but she would have to get over it. She got all her luck in life when she got me.

The old locals had watched us with suspicion as we walked into the pub. The general noise stopped and we were regarded by lots of eyes peering from under Neanderthal brows and shaggy eyebrows.

There was lots of counting on gnarled fingers as they worked out that there was a foreigner in their midst.

Looking at the open mouths and toothless gums as they reached that decision was like looking at Edvars Munch's The Scream in duplicate.

And, not just someone from outside the village was the verdict but a foreigner from faraway lands across the wide blue sea.

Lands that would take many, many, weeks of sailing to reach. Even in the fastest ships. Lands very near the edge of the saucer that was supported by four elephants. World's end.

They forgot about all that after Jan bought them a drink. Suddenly Jan was everyone's new best friend. There probably hadn't been this much excitement in the village since the Relief of Mafeking.

Everybody in the Red Lion toasted Adrian's engagement and forthcoming wedding. Even I pushed the boat out and had a double shandy.

Once the congratulations and good wishes were out of the way, everybody looked at me as if to say "Well. Go on then. Tell us."

Big Mick had already told Pete a little if what had happened yesterday. Not too much because he didn't know that much. Pete was the first to ask directly what had happened.

I took them back to the day that my trucker friend Clive had showed up at the allotment. When I had called in the favour he owed me.

I told them about plotting with Jan to let ET 'accidentally' see a box of vodka and a carton of fags being passed suspiciously, as if they were smuggled, from the back of the delivery truck.

How we guessed that he would make plans to get some for himself the next time he saw we had a delivery.

Once he had been spotted hanging about the shop and I saw the camera in his bedroom, we knew we had him.

I got Jan to make sure the next delivery driver rang him a day before coming to the shop.

When he rang, I got Jan to arrange for him to go to the A5 truckstop just outside Crick. He would be met there and goods and money would change hands. The driver agreed.

I phoned Clive and he showed up at the truck stop with his test truck and trailer. I joined him with the empty cartons I had picked up from Jan's shop the night before in my mpv.

I wasn't sure we really needed them but I thought they would be a bit of window dressing to make the trailer look more convincing.

Better too much than too little. Attention to detail and all that.

At the truck stop, the Polish delivery driver opened his rear doors. Clive opened his and I climbed into the back of the trailer.

The Polish driver backed slowly up to Clive's trailer until they touched each other's rubber bump strips.

The two trailers now formed a perfect bridge from one to the other.

It was easy then for me to use the driver's pump truck – a manually operated device for wheeling pallets about – and transfer Jan's delivery of two pallets into Clive's trailer. I pushed the pump truck back into the other trailer and then shouted for the trucks to separate.

Clive now had Jan's goods on board and would be the 'Polish' truck delivering to his shop. The Polish driver pocketed his £30 and was pleased with his end of the deal.

Instead of having the hassle of having to offload at Jan's shop, he could now continue on up the motorway to his next much easier delivery to a warehouse in Leeds.

Our little swop had saved him both the time and the effort of physically breaking down the two pallets and 'handballing' or manually transferring the contents into Jan's shop.

Jan reckoned that the £30 would buy the driver a nice house back in Poland. I wasn't sure whether he was joking or not.

All the talking had made my throat dry so Adrian got another round of drinks in. Just for us this time and not the salivating locals.

They were pointedly ignoring their game of drilled wood and matchsticks in favour of the spaniel eyes method of getting another free round.

No point in spoiling them. One or two of them were already sleeping under the tables. I could see sleeping bags and pillows stowed away under the bench seat some of them were sitting on. Maybe this was their home?

Another two were having a Zimmer frame fight loudly encouraged on by their ancient cronies. I ignored them and continued with my account of yesterday's activities to my, by now, rapt audience.

Once Clive had driven round to Jan's and parked up outside the shop, it was just a matter of waiting. They began unloading slowly and gave ET plenty of opportunity to see them and then get into the trailer.

Before long, much to their relief, they saw him walking up the road.

They saw him walk past then and observe them in the reflection from the computer shop's window.

Eventually he made his move and climbed into the back of the trailer. Jan and Clive rushed out and quickly shut the trailer doors. ET was trapped.

"Then what?" Big Mick asked. "You just park up or what?"

"No, you forget that Clive was testing an experimental engine on the truck and so he just carried on.

He normally has to drive two hundred or so miles a day so he just went off and did his normal route." I told them.

"The fact that he would be doing a night shift for a change didn't matter. It was just a matter of racking up the miles on the engine test."

"Well, weren't you worried about the kid hurting himself inside?" The ever practical Pete wanted to know.

"Not really. I put a couple of cameras in Clive's trailer about two years ago. He was doing a lot of work out of France and having problems with the immigrants waiting at Calais to cross over to the UK.

They would try to get into or even under trailers to smuggle themselves into England.

I fitted two cameras onto the trailer. One underneath and one inside the trailer. It gave him advance warning of the immigrants trying to get aboard

The cameras are those little infra –red jobs and they feed wirelessly to a monitor on his dash. He could watch ET inside the trailer all the time." I explained to the others.

"Well, wasn't he getting thrown about inside?" Big Mick asked. "Stuff used to get broken all the time in my trailers.

I'd sometimes get to my destination and there would be just matchsticks left."

"Yeah, well." I tried to be diplomatic. "Clive is a professional driver and gets paid a lot because he drives very smoothly. He had to have special training and everything." I said to mollify Big Mick.

"The trailer has special air suspension as well. It is all part of his job.

He sometimes carries very high value and fragile loads and the customer wouldn't be happy if anything was damaged or got broken."

Big Mick didn't look very impressed.

Eventually Clive observed ET fall into a restless sleep. He'd wake, walk about then go back to sleep again. He looked almost like he was sleep walking, Clive told me.

"Anyway, Clive did his usual route and eventually arrived back at the A5 truckstop. He'd had a couple of breaks during the night and there was no reaction from ET.

Clive had phoned me when he arrived and, after having his breakfast, went back to his truck and watched ET on the monitor."

He saw him walking about then trying to have a pee out of the gap in the trailer doors. He said that was funny.

Next he broke into one of the pallets and began eating from one of the cartons. He then rummaged around and found a tin of something.

"He was quite clever in using a piece of wood to puncture the can and get himself a drink of what we later found was pear syrup."

"But wasn't he cold at night?" Adrian asked. "It still gets parky at night and that trailer is all metal." He pointed out to the others.

"Not that cold as the trailer walls are insulated. Besides he made himself a shelter from some of the empty boxes I brought from Jan's shop." I told Adrian and the others.

"Actually Clive was quite impressed with how resourceful he was. He said he had a little cry a couple of times but did ok in what was meant to be a stressful situation."

"Didn't you feel bad about what you were doing to him?" Paul asked. He'd been quiet most of the time but, typically, asked the question that most concerned the others.

"Foo Kinell Paul." Jan said angrily. He looked around at us as if to remind us just who we were talking about.

"He did lots of bad things to me and my customers. The customers from the other shops as well. He and his friends are a bloody nuisance. They steal from the old people. He is not a nice boy."

" Yes, I felt a little bad." I told Paul. "But, then I remembered the little bugger slashed the tyres on my motor. Then I didn't feel too bad.

Besides, he's young and youngsters don't feel things like we do. You only have to look at them going to school in the middle of winter with no coats on to realise that."

"Yes, but he was also hungry and thirsty." Paul replied. "And that wasn't very nice for him."

"From what my grand daughter tells me about his home life, he's used to that. His mum is an alcoholic and spends her benefits on drink and fags.

The little bugger has had to fend for himself for a long time now. He's used to being hungry and thirsty."

"You sound like you're feeling sorry for him now" Adrian said quietly.

" I guess I am in a way. Brought up like that, he's had to look out for himself. Who's to say any of us wouldn't steal if we were hungry and thirsty?" I asked.

There were some sombre nods around the table.

"But, what happened then?" Pete wanted to know. "And whose round is it anyway?"

I looked around but knew it couldn't be helped. I'd been putting the moment off but knew it was finally time. I got up, went to the bar and bought a round of drinks.

That meant all the pocket money Lynne gives me was blown in one night. Bugger.

I guessed the question I asked earlier about what we would do if we were hungry and thirsty would be answered soon enough.

When everyone was sipping the drinks I had bought, I carried on. "Enjoy them, that's the last round I buy for a while." I warned.

"Bloody nectar." Adrian smiled. "And so unexpected."

"Don't push it you monotone old git or I'll tell Anya a few things about you that'll put her off for good." He just grinned back.

"Anyway Clive waited until he thought we were about ten minutes or so away and then went to the back of the trailer. He opened it and did his big angry foreign truck driver routine.

He doesn't speak Polish so shouted in German. He guessed that ET wouldn't know the difference anyway.

He fell for it and got really scared and blubbery. Particularly when Clive said he was taking him back to Poland so he could work off the damage to the stuff in the trailer.

Clive said he felt bad about that but carried on anyway.

When he saw Big Mick's van pulling up he pulled ET out by his feet, grabbed him by the shoulders and started shouting at him." They were all completely engrossed by now.

" I was driving and when I pulled up and I saw this big red haired bloke shaking this little kid, I got really angry." Big Mick joined in.

"Yeah, Jan had to hold onto him and remind him it was just an act." I almost laughed but felt it would spoil the atmosphere.

"Anyway, as arranged, Jan leapt out of the van and demanded that the driver let him go. The driver refused and they began slugging it out. Whilst they were 'fighting' I grabbed the kid and got him away. As soon as he was clear, Jan swung his big punch and knocked the driver out."

"Yah, it was a good fight." Jan laughed. "Good job he couldn't see how bad the punches really were. I pretended to give the driver a good kicking and then went back to the van. ET was so relieved he jumped out and hugged me. It was quite touching really."

I carried on. "Anyway Jan and the kid made friends. He gave ET a drink and an 'asprin' which put him to sleep and we just drove back to Jan's shop.

We left him sleeping in the van round the back of the shops and we then unloaded Clive.

He'd quickly recovered from his 'beating' and had followed us back. We unloaded the two pallets and he drove off. Now I owe him a favour." I told them. They all nodded seriously. They all knew about receiving and owing favours. It's a man thing.

"Hold on, back up a bit." Peter said suspiciously. "Go back to that 'gave ET an asprin which put him to sleep' bit again. What did you actually give him?" he looked at Jan for an answer.

"He gave him one of my Zopiclone sleeping tablets." I told him.

"It was only a low dose but, with all the stress and excitement, he went out like a light. It wouldn't affect him in any way. I checked first." I quickly assured them

"But, we didn't want him to know just where he was. After all, he's been driven around all night. He hadn't a clue where he was."

"Well, where did he think he was?" Adrian asked.

"Actually, very near where you were in Kent." This time I did laugh. "Jan kept an eye on him and when he woke up he took him into the shop.

He gave him a drink and a sandwich and told him the tale we had agreed.

About how I had phoned all my trucker friends and asked them to keep an eye out for the truck. How one had phoned back and said they'd seen it on the M20 pulling into the last service area before Dover."

Jan couldn't contain himself. " He thought he was on the way to Poland. We 'rescued' him and then drove him home. That's what he thinks had happened to him.

We didn't want him to know he was only a couple of miles from home so I gave him the pill.

When he woke up, he just thought he's been sleeping the whole way home."

There was a silence as they thought it through. Before long they were all laughing at how we'd conned a young lad into thinking he's been kidnapped and on his way to Poland for God knows what. Slavery or the sex trade?

Actually, put like that, it wasn't that funny and the laughter died away as we all realised it.

Adrian spoke for the rest of them. "Ok, I get why you did it and it must have been very convincing and scary for him. But, what now? What happens to the kid now? Is he just going to go back to his old ways?"

This was Jan's area and I let him get on with it. "I told him he had cost us a lot of money rescuing him.

The stuff from the trailer that he thinks I didn't get but would have to pay for. Plus the four tyres that he had slashed on Dave's car. The diesel for Mick's van going to Dover and back.

He said he'd pay us back. When I asked him how, he didn't know. I told him that he could work for me until he's earned enough to pay us all back.

He didn't like it but, I was surprised, he act like man, and agrees. So, from tomorrow, he works in my shop and helps me on the allotment. Is good, no?" Jan beamed at us.

Everyone did agree that the outcome was indeed good. We had a problem and we had dealt with it in our inimitable style.

Big Mick said it all when he raised his glass into the air. "The Allotmenteers," He said as we all touched, even Jan. "One for All and All for One."

He looked at Jan. "This doesn't mean you are one." He said. "Just this time." He warned him then asked.

" By the way, when am I going to get my diesel money back? It's a long way to Kent and back in my old van. It cost me a fair bit in diesel."

No body said anything. He was being serious. We just looked at each other.

Chapter Thirty Eight.

April and May just seemed to fly by. Everything does when you are getting to recycling age. But, those two months on the allotment are always busy times.

There is always lots to do. There's planting out and bringing on stuff in the green house before transferring outside. Keeping thermal covers ready in case of a sudden cold snap. Getting bird and butterfly protection nets and their poles ready. The other 101 jobs that have to get done before you can finally relax.

I'd go down in the early morning and weed. After a cuppa and my enjoyment of a new day, of course.

Adrian didn't join me so much these days. I missed our morning chats but he had now had a new friend to chat with in the mornings.

He was spending a lot of time getting things sorted out at Anya's house in Kent. They were hoping she could have finalised things down there and move to Rugby before their wedding on the first Saturday in June.

The rest of us keep his plot up to scratch and to planting timetables while he is otherwise occupied.

Jan was spending more time down the allotment as well. He had got into the habit of coming for a morning coffee but did provide me with a jar of some decent Polish stuff.

And, after trying my grey milk power mix, added several tins of evaporated milk from his shop as well. I grudgingly accepted them.

So, I was gradually sliding back into the hell of coffee addiction. I'd probably be smoking next and then driving away in big shiny trucks.

Strangely I don't miss the trucking too much now. I did at first but I always have my memories fall back on. Although locating them in my mental storage facilities is sometimes an almost impossible task.

Lynne keeps telling me, with a mixture of glee and impatience, that I am getting old.

She is always trying to confuse me with questions about wills, provisions for her and the kids, funeral costs and how will she survive without me.

I am never quite sure whether she means emotionally or financially.

But the allotment gets me out of the house which was the initial attraction. That it now provides me with an interest in life, good friends and produce that is slowly getting up to Aldi standards is a bonus.

Lynne still comes down when the weather is nice. She has threatened to make it more regular and intends to paint allotment scenes when the summer finally arrives. Whether I will still enjoy the allotment so much then is debateable.

Thankfully she and the other Allotmenteers wives are occupied getting themselves worked up about Adrian's and Anya's wedding.

She asked me the other day if I knew where she could hire out some chickens. She has this idea of the chickens walking up the aisle behind the happy couple to give an 'atmospheric' feel. Personally the only chickens I hoped to see on the day would be naked and on plates.

But, the biggest surprise was also turning out to be quite a success story. The tearaway boy we 'rescued from a fate worse than death' was growing up into a really nice young man.

Ethan, he doesn't like being called ET these days, is still working at Jan's shop. From what Jan tells me, he and his wife Irenka have pretty much adopted him.

He comes for his breakfast, Mrs Jan packs him a lunchbox for school - going back to school was also part of the deal – and he eats with them in the shop flat in the evening.

He has gone from being skinny to nicely filled out. He always looks clean and tidy whenever I see him at the shop or on the allotment.

Irenka makes sure he get regular showers at the shop and makes sure his clothes are washed and pressed. I think she also buys him new stuff although Jan doesn't mention this.

He comes down the allotment with Jan as well. Jan tells him what to do but also tells him why he is doing it.

I think Jan also looks upon him as a son – his own are married and still in Poland – and is trying to bring him up as a good Polish citizen.

I even heard the two of them talking in Polish and laughing with each other the other day and had the thought that Jan, Irenka and Ethan were good for each other.

The end of last month he came down to my shed and handed over an envelope. It contained £280 to pay for my replacement tyres. He apologised and I accepted his apology.

We got talking and I found him to be an articulate and, dare I say it, quite a likeable young man.

I asked him about the shop and he said he liked working there. Jan and Irenka were good to him, treated him very well, didn't work him too hard and paid him fairly.

I gathered he still slept at home but spent most of his time voluntarily at the shop. I asked him what his former friends thought of his 'conversion'.

He said they had initially thought it to be a scam he was running. When they found out it wasn't, some of them left the crew but the others still used to hang around the shops at night.

With Ethan keeping them under control, the situation was different now. The music got a bit loud sometimes but Ethan made sure it was quiet after 9.30 in deference to the old folk opposite.

Jan had told me that the situation outside the shops was now acceptable.

The other surprise was when he mentioned that Linzi, my grand daughter, said that I might be able to help him with an idea he had.

I was surprised that Linzi had kept quiet that she was even talking to Ethan. The other was that his idea was quite a good one.

Ethan had noticed that there were several empty plots. He found that he enjoyed working down the allotments and was interested in plants and stuff.

He had toyed with the idea of seeing if he could get a plot for himself but had then expanded the idea.

Talking to some of his old gang about what he was doing and why had sparked an interest in some of the others. He had asked Jan if he could take them down to see the allotments and Jan had accompanied them.

Once down there it soon became clear to Jan that they seemed genuinely interested. They asked some intelligent questions about the plot and what sort of vegetables and 'stuff' could be grown.

Jan explained that England was too cold to grow cannabis outdoors. Also that there was no electricity on the allotments. They took it well.

Some even asked if they could come down and help him and Ethan at the weekends sometimes.

Jan, knowing that I knew someone at the Town Hall, had told him to have a word with me. Sensibly, he waited until he thought I would be in a good mood to ask me.

Receiving £280 had put me in a good mood so I listened to his idea.

Basically he wanted to know how the council would react to a youth club taking over a plot? With proper adult supervision he pointed out, meaning Jan but also looking pointedly at me, but a plot they could look after themselves and be responsible for.

The first thought at the back of my head was 'who are you and what have you done with that ET toerag?' But, I could see lots of advantages behind the idea.

It would get the kids off the street and doing something useful. They might even learn something about where their food came from. It would be healthy with exercise and fresh air thrown in. I could see no real negatives at all.

I told him that I would ask John Burns the Park and Open Spaces manager for his initial thoughts.

If he said it was worth considering then there would have to be a meeting down at the allotments. Not only between Ethan, his friends and John Burns but the other allotment holders as well. However, I couldn't see the other guys having any objections so long as there was proper supervision and the kids were serious.

Personally, I was optimistic and I told him I thought it was a great idea and he should get some of his ideas and thoughts on paper for the meeting.

"Linzi said you might be able to help me with that, Grumps. She says you are good with words and stuff." He told me.

"Whoa… whoa, back up a minute there. What did you just call me?"

He thought back and his face went red. "Sorry mister. It's just that I'm so used to Linzi calling you Grumps that I think of you that way too. I won't do it again."

Was there something serious going on between Ethan and Linzi, I wondered? And, more importantly, was I worried? The initial reaction from my gut was a firm No. I could think of worse guys for her. And, a few weeks back I didn't think I would ever be happy with that scenario.

The allotment had worked its magic again. "Naw, that's all right, son. You can call me Grumps if you like. But, not in front of the old wrinkleys ok?"

He grinned until I added "But if you hurt Linzi or mess her about then you and I will have words. Serious words. Is that clear?"

He said he got the message. Told me to 'chilax' what ever that meant.

Chapter Thirty Nine.

May had been an odd month. There was lots of unseasonable sunshine, freeze your ass off nights and a few days of very heavy rain. Everyone was glad that June was nearly here.

"There's no bloody sign of them." Big Mick moaned. He and Paul were standing at the end of his allotment studying a patch of bare earth. " I'm not too bothered about the other stuff but I was hoping to grow something from the Greggs seeds."

It was the patch that Big Mick had laboriously dug when he was planting his 'experimental' gift seeds.

Paul had watched him go up daily and look for any signs of growth for two or three weeks now. He had dug so deep that even the weeds hadn't started growing yet.

After every negative inspection he had trudged dejectedly back, into his shed and consoled himself with the stuff he was expecting to grow.

"Yeah, looks like the birds got them. They must have got the taste from the crumbs around your shed." Paul had managed to say with a straight face.

Apart from that one patch of bare earth there wasn't much else to show that the plot was being rented or worked. The complete comparison between Big Micks 'natural' plot and Paul's meticulously maintained one couldn't have been more obvious.

"Yeah, but how is it that stuff grows for you and everyone else?" Big Mick continued. "What's the secret?"

How long have you got, Paul thought to himself. "Some people have green fingers and some don't." he said diplomatically. "You just have to keep at it to get the results."

"Yeah well, I still think those bloody seeds were rubbish."

They were a strange couple. The big guy and the thin one. But, like most opposites, they rubbed along together.

Paul wasn't into much conversation and he liked that Big Mick's badly neglected plot showed his own off to its best advantage.

"Bit late to get anything in now apart from some winter greens."

"I was hoping to grow some flowers for the wedding." Big Mick told his neighbour. "Looks like I'll have to buy some now. Do you think Adrian will notice?"

"Oh, he's bound to. Shop flowers can never really match up to home grown. I can let you have some of mine though if you're stuck." Paul offered.

The wedding seemed to be the main topic of conversation for everyone. It seemed that everyone on the Victory Allotments were united in wishing the happy couple well.

*****

"I'm not wearing a dickey bow." I told Lynne firmly. " It makes me look like an old man."

"I've got news for you. You are an old man so get it on."

I was bloody glad I wasn't getting married again. Being old White Hair's best man was proving both trying and expensive enough.

Why I had to have a brand new suit, I didn't know. I had already seen a nice one in the Myton Hospice charity shop. It was a little large but it could have been altered. Let the trousers out a bit. Maybe shorten the sleeves.

I took Lynne in to show it to her. I found myself being marched off to Berton's for a new off the peg in beige. Beige! I'd be getting a bloody matching cardigan next.

"It looks very nice." She told me as I came out of the changing room. She had her hand up to her mouth as she said it through a coughing fit.

Actually it wasn't bad but I wasn't going to tell her that. I had a new white shirt on and she had chosen a flowery bow tie for me to try. It was one of those old man clip on types.

The white shirt and beige suit did show off my newly acquired deep tan to its best advantage though.

I tan easily and the last few weeks working outside on the allotment had given me a Costa Hillmorton tan. And, unlike my truck driving days, both arms were the same colour.

In a truck only one arm ever gets tanned. You can tell whether a trucker drives a left or right hand drive truck simply by looking at his arms. Well, it *might* be useful if you are stuck sometime. You never know.

"We'll have it." Lynne told the Berton's guy. " We'll put it away after the wedding. Save it for your funeral." She wasn't joking.

The Bertons guy gave me a sympathetic look behind her back.

Then he probably thought of his commission and wasn't bothered. There is just no real bond between men anymore. Sold out for a measly forty pieces or £120.

"Right, that's you sorted. Now to see if I can find something to wear."

I pointed out that she had wardrobes full of stuff. She counter pointed out that it was stuff she had worn before.

Therefore she would be getting something new for herself. We went to Marks and Spencer. She choose something floral and expensive.

 She went straight to it so I guessed it was all planned beforehand. She made to get her debit card out then thought better of it. "It can be your treat to thank me for finding your suit." she said. "Thank you Darling. I love it."

"You're welcome my little princess." I managed to get out through the lump in my throat and the moths flying from my wallet.

*****

In his garage cum workshop, Pete was putting the finishing touches to an elegant long case clock. He had bought it some time ago in a 'not working' condition and had spent a lot of time getting it to do so.

The actual case was in very good condition and needed nothing other than a bit of elbow grease and some wood polish.

Standing in the garage with its newly repaired innards ticking quietly away, it looked as if it had been made yesterday and not over a hundred years ago.

Pete hoped that Anya and Adrian liked it. He liked the 'personal touch' gifts himself and he hoped the happy couple did as well.

Where it would end up hadn't been decided yet as neither Anya or Adrian had decided to leave finding a new home, if at all, until after the honeymoon. But for now, he liked having it in his garage. He found it very soothing listening to it.

He couldn't believe how quickly the time had gone. Only two more days now and it would all be over.

It would be nice to get back to a more normal routine once all the wives had calmed down.

Get back down the allotment and chat with the others whilst the wives all thought they were all working hard.

Just what was it about women and weddings he wondered?

And, just why did so many people put themselves through that ordeal more than once?

Maybe it was like his thrice married sister had jokingly said. "I'm addicted to wedding cake."

Chapter Forty.

I can't believe it is nearly the end of September already. Where has the year gone? One minute you are thinking of planting. The next your storehouse is full and the neighbours make excuses when they are offered more potatoes, cabbages and stuff. Oh well, their loss. Come the Food Crash, they'll wish they had taken it.

That is the only problem with an allotment. You tend to grow more than you can actually eat, store or use.

Consequently you give lots away to family, friends, neighbours and even complete strangers you pass in the street. "You want a cabbage, mate? There you go, enjoy."

It had been a bountiful year on the allotment. Well, apart from on one solitary plot where the advertised goods definitely weren't produced.

Big Mick asked me to write a letter of complaint to the seed company that 'sent' him the experimental seeds. He wanted recompense in lieu of his hard labour. He got a hand delivered reply apologising and promising to send him some even more exotic seeds next year.

The wedding? Oh yeah, the wedding. That went off very well, thank you. Adrian looked beautiful. Anya looked gorgeous. The Best man stole the show. The Maid of Honour well, she wasn't a maid and clearly hadn't been for some time.

The bride arrived in the latest model Rolls Royce courtesy of the PR Director who owed me a favour from around five years ago.

He tried to get out of it at first but, eventually common decency and respect for the sacred Favour shone through. It's a Man Thing.

Now I owe him one once more. Let's just hope it doesn't involve wives, bowls and car keys again.

Fortunately Lynne failed to procure the chickens so the bride was walked down the aisle accompanied only by a beaming Pete.

Anya looked a bit confused as she saw two old men in beige suits waiting for her. Both deeply tanned and both with white hair. But, with a bit of Eeny Meney Mo, she eventually got the right guy.

It took ages for the white to go from my hair. I'd got some white temporary colour spray off Ebay. It looked ok at the altar but, at the reception it started to run as the heat built up.

But, as the next time I would be wearing that suit had already been decided, it didn't really matter.

They left the church to a guard of Allotmenteers holding up long handled hoes for them to walk under.

Some of the guys had even changed their clothes before attending. Big Mick hadn't.

But he did bring his wife and it became very evident just why he spent so much time down the allotment. Opposites attracting again. He big boned, she stick thin. He happy and jovial, she not. They both left halfway through the reception arguing away happily.

The happy couple intended to have a couple of days away at Blackpool before doing some serious house hunting. Apparently it was one of Anya's dream destinations. She had always wanted to stay at a Blackpool guest house, meet a real live Blackpool landlady and have tea and a dance in the Tower. Foreigners eh?

The Roller was going back to it's Crewe HQ so we had a quick whip round and gave the driver a fuel donation for a slight detour. In return we promised not to tie anything to the back of the car.

When they got back, by train, two days later, tanned and even more tanned, they had already decided about housing.

Adrian didn't really want to leave his current place. Not just because of the memories it held for him but also because of its convenient back gate entrance to his allotment.

Anya hadn't felt any bad vibes from the house or its former mistress so felt comfortable about staying on. Besides, she could see her daughter Kinga's memorial garden from Adrian's' kitchen window. It seemed stupid to move anywhere else.

They jointly decided on an extra room in the roof and extending outwards as many of their neighbours had done.

Currently the building work is coming along nicely. They hope to be completed, redecorated and refurnished before Christmas.

Adrian had promised us that we can occasionally use the hot tub he has planned for the decking. He said we have to remove our wellies first though. He didn't say anything about using his solarium. They are still both very happy. Anya the most.

Lynne is the same. She is at her happiest when spending money as well. Well, we are not moving and definitely not having a hot tub on the decking. I'm not sure it'll stand the weight and the Glums need some time off from their ever constant vigil.

She finally settled for an outside blind over the french windows, with an outside handle winder in and outer. Also for some posh decking lights. I have put them both down on the To Do List. Something for me to do during the long dark winter months. I'll get to them. …..Eventually.

So reflections on another year on the allotments are far more pleasant than those upsets of last year. And out of their joint unhappiness Adrian and Anya now have found something special. So that has been a positive.

The one negative of this year for me has been losing my little Yorkie Penny. It's been some time now and I still miss her. I guess I will always have a place for her in my heart.

Another positive has been Ethan Turner aka ET. The change in this guy has been epic. Due largely, I think, to Jan and Irenka Hawkn'spit's joint input.

Regular food, a stable and caring environment, a bit of TLC and people he now looks up to have completely transformed this former tearaway.

Now you'd be proud to know he is, as Facethingy officially put it 'in a relationship', - whatever that means and what I hope it doesn't mean - with your oldest grand daughter. I know I am that he is with mine.

His youth group allotment idea was, after a lot of discussion and on a trial basis, given permission.

The council donated two adjoining plots, fenced and rotovated them, put a decent shed up and basically said "Now do us and yourselves proud." And the little buggers did just that.

What was more, many of the older plot holders were grudgingly roped in as advisors and mentors.

It was great to see the distrust and hostilities from both sides, young and old, gradually thaw and combine into mutual trust, appreciation and friendships.

Given the tensions and the attitudes that existed last year and now to regularly hear laughter and to see happy people on the Victory Allotments is like a minor miracle.

Nor has it stopped there. Ethan and Linzi have taken to visiting the residents of the old folks home as well. The manager was a bit unsure at first but gave permission for a limited time trial with only them involved.

Now at least twenty of the local youth visit at least twice a week, many daily, and chat to the old folk. It is an education for both sides of the age bracket as they chat and learn from each other.

The youngsters tend to open up about home and life issues to someone who isn't involved, has time to listen and who can give good advice as well.

They get a new perspective on their lives and how much different those lives might have turned out if not for the courage, sacrifice and stoicism of these once mocked, ridiculed or just ignored old folk.

The old told the young of wartime tragedies, food and clothes shortages ands how hard things really were.

The youngsters replied with tales of no phone signals, no credit and lost internet connections and how hard things really were.

They learnt how things used to be before electronics, tvs and the internet. In the old days when everything was black and white.

The old relived their youth through today's youth. And, hopefully, passed on the hard earned lessons of their lives back to them as well.

Some of the old ladies taught the boys the basics of dance. The Waltz, the Foxtrot and the Hokey Cokey. Remembering old dreams, loves and lovers as they once more held firm young bodies in their arms.

The youngsters, with varying degrees of success, are teaching the wrinkleys to use computers. It is expected to take some time.

But the joy and excitement on their old faces as some of them send an email to a grandchild or surf the internet for the first time more than makes up for the time, frustration and patience shown by their young tutors.

The youngsters clearly filled a void with their happy chatter, interest, questions and youthful exuberance. They brought new life into a world largely dominated by old faces.

The manager of the Home, seeing the changes, declared the trial a success.

Some of the more mobile residents, together with their young companions, even caught the bus from the stop over the road and got off three stops later and walked to the nearby Victory Allotments.

They entered and you could almost see the allure and life force of the allotment take them over. It was like the film Cocoon all over again.

The few became many as word in the home spread.

Soon the queue for the bus became of almost comic proportions. Eventually the manager had to resort to a shuttle service using the Home's mini bus.

He did it willingly as the change in those in his care became more and more apparent.

The Home was almost overnight transformed from God's Dreary Waiting Room to a place of fun, music and laughter.

And, it later transpired, an award winning example of just how an Old Folks Home should be run.

So any troubled conscience or doubts we may have had about the sharp, hard, knock we gave to Ethan have long since gone. Now we Allotmenteers can bask in the glow of another successful mission.

Everything is rosy on the Victory Allotments. Another year grows to an end and we all, young and old alike, look forward to the next one with enthusiasm and anticipation.

Apart from the one fly that may be soon landing in the ointment, that is.

With their house alterations finished and the interior completely redone, Adrian and Anya took them selves off to Fuengirola in Spain for a fortnight's sun, sand, sea and we'll see how I feel laters.

He rang me up after the first week. "Hey
Dave…. Yes, it's me… Adrian you old fool,
who's you think?…Yes, we are both ok and
enjoying ourselves….Yes the weather is very
hot……You've got rain?

…We'd love a drop of rain to bring the heat
down…..no seriously, it's too hot. Look, I'm
ringing to tell you something….if you give
me a minute, I'll get to it. Look, let me tell it
in my own way all right? We were on a coach
trip to Seville and you'll never guess who we
ran into in a bar there………..Well try, you'll
never get it in a million years.

No, it wasn't… that one is spelt S.A. and
he's dead….well   a few years back now….
Didn't you hear about all the scandal?

Give up? …ok it was Albert Collins… Yeah,
our Bert Collins. Of all the bars in all the
world and I had to walk into that one right?
….Neither of us could believe it…He went
white….

No, I didn't tell Anya…well why do you
think?...she'd   have   killed   him…..Well,
maybe but then we wouldn't get home for a
long time………

Well, he is here in Spain, …yes, it's
definitely him…. he gave me a message for
you and the others as he walked past to the
door…… He says he will be back and he will
get even… Yes, he included you…..because
he called you an old trucker…Yes I am sure
he said trucker…. yes, he looked very
serious.

No, by the time I contacted the police he had gone…just disappeared….yes, they are looking…well, it's a big place and they didn't find him before did they?…… The question is……do you think he was serious about coming back and getting even?…..

Do you think he will be back?………"

?

Author's note.

Enough of a cliff hanger for you? I hope you enjoyed this follow up to The Allotment! If you did, can you please write a Review for me? To let me know how you feel I am doing.

Speaking of reviews, my thanks to all the people who took the time to write those nice reviews for The Allotment!

Also the people who contacted me by email to say how much they enjoyed my book.

They gave me the incentive and enthusiasm to write this sequel.

It is nice to know that I can make people laugh and that all the time I spend writing a book isn't wasted. Writing is a lonely business sometimes and constructive criticism is always welcome as a barometer of how I am doing.

As you may know I also write the John Slater books about trucking for truckdrivers.

John Slater: The Journey and John Slater: The German Job are currently available on Amazon in paperback and Kindle format.

My Oh Grumps! range of children's books are also available at Amazon in paperback and Kindle as well.

You will note that I write these under a different pen name. This is to differentiate between the three genres: Trucking, Children's and Allotment.

Because I am under pressure to write a new John Slater book and my grand daughter Tilly wants a new Oh Grumps! book with her new sister in it, this is the last of The Allotment! books for awhile.

But, I like writing the Allotment books and there are plenty more ideas and stories to write about later on.

Hopefully I'll be able to start a new one later this year.

In the meantime, I really would welcome your reviews and thoughts on all my books. Try them. You never know, you might like them. My weird sense of humour is present in all of them, even the Children's.

You can email me at
dwfurlong@talktalk.net

The author has been an international truckdriver and owner driver. He became a transport journalist for national and international magazines. He was also a development driver for new and experimental vehicles, drivelines and ancillary equipment.

He is now retired – but working harder than ever it seems - and tends for his allotment, kids, grandkids and Yorkie dogs. He lives in Rugby with his long suffering wife Lynne.

He doesn't do Facethingy or Twatter!

Where the magic happens

Not only Adrian who has white hair now.

Printed in Great Britain
by Amazon

81702890R00180